MW00937321

The Wizard's
HANDBOOK

How to Be a Wizard in the 21st Century

Mario Garnet

Cover Art by Tamara Starr
Illustrations by Tamara Starr & Alice Domineske

BALBOA.
PRESS
A DIVISION OF HAY HOUSE

Balboa Press books may be ordered through booksellers or by contacting:

Balboa Press
A Division of Hay House
1663 Liberty Drive
Bloomington, IN 47403
www.balboapress.com
1-(877) 407-4847

ISBN: 978-1-4525-3608-8 (sc)
ISBN: 978-1-4525-3611-8 (hc)
ISBN: 978-1-4525-3612-5 (e)

Library of Congress Control Number: 2011911036

Because of the dynamic nature of the Internet, any web addresses or links contained in this book may have changed since publication and may no longer be valid. The views expressed in this work are solely those of the author and do not necessarily reflect the views of the publisher, and the publisher hereby disclaims any responsibility for them.

The author of this book does not dispense medical advice or prescribe the use of any technique as a form of treatment for physical, emotional, or medical problems without the advice of a physician, either directly or indirectly. The intent of the author is only to offer information of a general nature to help you in your quest for emotional and spiritual well-being. In the event you use any of the information in this book for yourself, which is your constitutional right, the author and the publisher assume no responsibility for your actions.

Printed in the United States of America

Balboa Press rev. date: 07/07/2011

To my granddaughters Ashley & Chloe

&

Tamara's Son, Devin

And

The growing population of Quantum thinkers.

Epigraph:

Be MORE than you can be!

Think out of the Box

Contents

List of Illustrations

Preface

The magical life of Harry Potter in J.K. Rowling's Series intrigues us for it triggers something deep within the recesses of our soul. We know that the magical world is real somehow and that it is THIS earthly world which is limited. We know it is our destiny to tap into the powers within us and create a world without limits.

It is our goal to present to the seeker a grander awareness of who we are and the powers we actually do have by presenting both the magic inherent in our current human culture as well as the mystical truths still hidden from the majority.

For optimum results it is best to read the Grottos slowly in sequential order.

This book is assigned to

_____.

Acknowledgements

Special thanks to my wife Pat Seimes for steering me in the right direction and for her collaboration, support, and input.

To my daughter, Alasan Pfluger for her endearing support and suggestions. To Gabriella Payne-Tomafsky, for being my youngest advocate and to Calvin North as an inspiration of our future.

To Karen Seimes for her psychic intervention that generated the production process of this book.

To Donna Gudauskas, friend and professional copy editor who critiqued and cradled my manuscript.

Special thanks to the following as inspiration for the characters: Sam & Anita Carney as themselves; Gedi Gudauskas for Professor Gustaf; Pat Seimes as Sister Sulis; my 10th grade history teacher Mr. Henderson as himself, and Dr. Robin M. Levin, as Dr. Oiseau. And, of course, JK Rowling's *Dumbledore* for Headmaster Muhlaton. The concept of the dragon came from BBC's television show *Merlyn*.

Special thanks to long time associate Howard Rosenbloom for encouraging me to expand, to Luke ('Skyfall') Hart for reminding me how to feel, and Professor Joe Diaco for his insights into our educational system.

And for a wonderful Editorial Staff at Balboa Press for their encouragement and professionalism: Teresa Nicodemus, Echo Fluharty, Jennifer Slaybaugh, Janelle Gonyea, and the rest of the staff.

And finally for all contacts past present and future who have influenced me in positive ways.

The Journey

Let's grab our imaginary broomsticks and glide through Disney's® Wizarding World of Harry Potter™ in Hogsmeade where we see a gathering of novice wizards under an archway atop a balcony platform overlooking Hogwarts Castle. Behind us is the landmark owl and wizard statue.

The group seems to be listening to someone. Aha! It appears to be Headmaster Muhlaton of the Virtual School of Wizardry (a learn-at-home discourse). He is a tall lean man with very little hair on top, sporting a goatee of sorts. Wearing a multicolored gown of light, he speaks in a low but projecting voice, the kind that demands attention yet offers solace. Let us hear what he is saying ...

"Fellow students of life and magic, both new and ancient souls, it is with great pleasure I invite you to explore your possibilities as we journey together through the many Grottos of our virtual school, learning about the many magical features of our world and the powers within you. I am Headmaster Muhlaton and will be your guide through this journey. Since our group has grown to twelve, we may proceed. Please be seated."

As he says this, twelve chairs each of a different color with smiling faces on the backs, waddle (with flexible legs) onto the platform. As we each sit on a uniquely colored living chair, the chairs separate from the group and float on individual circular platforms; we jettison as an assembly into a swirling multi-colored pillar of light.

Soon we find ourselves descending and then hovering above a half circle stage while the Headmaster glides to the front of the stage with eight vaporous dynamos around him. "Welcome to the first stage of your journey—our introductory ceremony. After I introduce each Grotto's instructor you may follow him or her to their classroom. On my left is Mr. Henderson. He will be in charge of Grotto 101. With him you will learn about the evolution of the human world in preparation for the subsequent magical studies".

The Headmaster introduces Mr. Henderson--but, there is no Mr. Henderson—only a ball of light. Then sure enough the ball forms into a large black skinned man, a bit large around the middle with a broad smile and a mysterious twinkle in his eye; yet, his entire figure seems to fade in and out like a hologram trying to solidify. Finally after his image is well entrained in our brains, Mr. Henderson vanishes into the mist.

As we re-focus our eyes on Master Muhlaton, he says, "To my right, I present Sister Sulis. This year she will teach Grotto 102 in place of Samantha who is teaching abroad in Lithuania at our sister school."

Unexpectedly, a green puddle appears next to Muhlaton. As we watch, it expands upward, like melting in reverse, to form a shape of a green woman with a green head, atop of which strands of bright red hair squirm down to her waist like a hundred snakes. The little mole on her nose, though, seemed to be a bit out of sorts.

Meeting at Hogsmeade (T. Starr)

ster Sulis comes to us from a long line of noble Celtic s. She will clear up the matter of witches and wizards to everyone's satisfaction I am sure." As she eyed us, we could feel the shudders pass through the group. She abruptly returns to her puddle state.

As the Headmaster nods to his left, all we can see is a giant silver egg, about 5 feet high. A large crack grows on the egg from top to bottom and out steps a most interesting creature while the Headmaster announces: "From the 'land of healthy beings' I hereby present Mademoiselle Docteur Robyn Oiseau, teacher of the magical human body in Grotto 103."

Robyn Oiseau is the most beautiful creature we had ever seen, her angel face radiant with a bright green light, her eyes flashing like green emeralds, and a pair of luminous snow white wings on her delicate shoulders. The epitome of health, she exits from her shell (actually some kind of spaceship) wearing a white fluffy robe of feathers that intertwines with her wings.

Finally when the Headmaster could break his stare, he declares: "Doctor Oiseau flew in from the 5th dimension world to share with you the known secrets of the human vessel--your bodies. I trust you will give her your full attention since her wisdom is infused in all successful wizards." Dr. Oiseau flaps her wings and flies into the tapestry of the sky and disappears from sight.

The Headmaster continues: "Our fourth instructor is Professor Gustaf von Lichtenstein. In Grotto 104, the Magic of the Universe, he will take you on a journey of the universe few have seen, of dimensions and possibilities at the edge of human awareness."

As we watch the Headmaster speak, to our right we see the wall of air open as if there were a zipper and, with a loud crack of electricity, emerges the grand Professor Gustaf, in appearance a combination of Einstein, Hawkins, and Sagan all wrapped as one. He has a serene youthful face emblazed with a full silvery well-trimmed illustrious beard and a full head of matching silver hair. He bows with reverence with his fists folded toward his chest, much like a martial arts sensei would. He then steps aside of the Headmaster who continues: "Yes there is magic in the real world. But, YOU do not live in the real world; you live in a limited world constrained by time and space which is projected from the real world much like a two dimensional photograph is taken in a three dimensional world."

"Together we will show *you* how magic appears in this world, often as science, often as not, as well as some of the magic techniques that are known only by few, handed down from secret societies, private witches and wizards, indigenous cultures, and the pagan worlds."

> *"The true wizard is the human who understands his/her world in its many manifestations and wields control of his/her own life."*

"For Grotto 105, I will be your Professor as I explain to you the techniques of magic. We will then culminate our work and practice magic together in the Illuminato Session."

In a flash, the Headmaster Muhlaton and Professor Gustaf vanish along with the stage and we find ourselves suddenly in Grotto 101.

The Instructors (T. Starr)

Grotto 101:
Magic of Knowledge

From the open sky above we hear Mr. Henderson speak in a booming voice, "Greetings!" To everyone's amazement, the only thing we can see on the stage is a large brown dragon with a ferocious face and wings outstretched. A stream of hot fire pours out of his snout as he rotates his head staring intently towards all the students, eye to eye, practically scorching our faces. He is looking at <u>us</u>. Startled, it is difficult to stay seated. Even the smiley living chairs are shaking their feet.

While counting to 12—1, 2, 3 …., the dragon focuses into the souls of each student. He says with a slow drawl and deeply resonating low pitched voice: "I see you have the spirit and have entered my world," stretching his long snout, revealing very large teeth.

"We have lived on this planet for many, many centuries and are known in your history books as dinosaurs. We have enjoyed this planet without humans for a long, LOOONG time. Even in your time, humans still have trouble believing we could fly and spit fire." He laughs so hard, his giant belly shakes while tiny balls of fire spout out forming a halo above his head in the shape of a dodecahedron.

Another dragon approaches the stage from the left with two baby-sized dragons. The ferocious looking dragon suddenly modifies his expression to a soft almost cute face, lips curling around his teeth almost hiding them, as he exclaims in his proud parent voice: "Oh, this is my family—as you can see I have two young ones, Dino and Din Ella."

It is clear Mr. Dragon (who calls himself Fragenard) is proud of his family. Approaching his partner Phoebe, they rub faces; then he kisses his two children. As Fragenard sends his family off to do whatever dragon families do, he slowly morphs back into Mr. Henderson, the shape shifter.

"We really do not know much about human history on this planet until written records actually appeared. We consider the days of the Roman Empire, Greek Antiquities, and Egyptian Pharaohs as our Ancient History. Since there was such an impact from these ancient cultures upon the many states of Europe, we have consequently inherited much of these cultures into our modern way of life."

As Mr. Henderson changes into a Roman wearing a white Toga down to his sandals, he says: "I am a little known Roman Senator Marius Gallius. I am acknowledged as an important citizen of Rome. My wife and children live on our estate near the outskirts of the city. While she manages the household and the education of our children, I give speeches and present arguments for my clients in Roman court. I am in this position because I was able to get a good education in the required courses of rhetoric, grammar, music, Latin, logic, arithmetic, geometry and astronomy. Rhetoric, as you can guess, is critical in my field—it is the art of persuasion using logic. And knowledge of geometry sharpens my intelligence. Our empire has created many things including roads to help move food and products among our many villages and cities, a viaduct to move water to our homes, a sewer system to keep the land clean, and schools to educate our young which you all enjoy thousands of years later."

While we ponder that thought, the good Senator morphs into a Greek student. "Health to You. I am Matrica, a student of mysteries. You can't imagine how exciting it is here in Greece to wake up each morning, greet the Sun as it rises, and attend the Pythagorean Secret School. Ssshh! Most people would be upset at what Pythagoras is teaching. It is the ultimate in new thinking. He believes that numbers reveal the order of nature. We play with this idea by experimenting with musical tones and octaves of musical scale. We learn, in fact, that the entire universe is based upon numbers. He calls it the 'Music of the Spheres'."

"One of Pythagoras' favorite topics is geometry and the sacred nature of geometric shapes. The number 3 represents the sacred triangle for which we have special reverence. One type of triangle demonstrates the 'Pythagorean Theorem', the one with a right angle–you know–where the area of the hypotenuse equals the area of each of the sides. That is really magical. We even learned how to use it in building and designing things."

Mr. Henderson morphs briefly as himself and interjects: "As simple as this theorem seems to 21st century students, Einstein expanded it into 'Einstein's Hypotenuse' while developing a method to understand multiple dimensions. Wait till you attend Professor Gustaf's Grotto!"

Matrica quickly returns and continues, "We also learned that the Babylonians much earlier in time had already understood much about numbers and shapes. Did you know that they counted using <u>both</u> their fingers and toes? That means when they get to the twentieth toe they start over. For example, our '25' which is based on counting with ten fingers means counting the ten fingers twice and adding five fingers. Now try counting using ten fingers <u>and</u> ten toes; you count all twenty digits ONE time and then start over beginning with the first finger counting up to five fingers. So that number would be written as one set plus five or fifteen (15). Seems confusing? Not to them."

Magic of History (A. Domineske)

Watching him chattering about numbers this way and that way, he was beginning to turn into Alice's Mad Hatter. "I can remember when Alice said 'Four times five is twelve... Oh Dear, I will never get to twenty.' She was not being stupid or confused; she was just speaking in a different numbering system language that is based on eighteen fingers", explained Mr. Henderson, popping in. "The '1' in '12' represents ONE set of eighteen fingers while the '2' equals two single fingers, so it is written as one set of eighteen digits plus two single digits or twelve (12). Perhaps they did not have thumbs!"

Mr. Henderson adds: "You can also count using only your thumbs—representing 0 and 1. Counting one thumb is a single 1, but counting the second thumb you have to add a zero and move the 1 over. So two becomes '10' ; then adding the next thumb you count one set of thumbs plus one or 10 plus 1 resulting in '11' which is actually three in our system of 10. Can you see how twenty might be 10100 counting in thumbs? Sound silly? In your time period the tribe that uses thumbs is called the *Geeks*.

[Author's Hint: the one's and zero's are place holders for multiples of two's increasing from right to left; in this case 10100 has the place holders of 16, 8, 4, 2, and 1 wherein only two places are filled with a number other than zero--the positions of '16' and '4' meaning there are no values in the '0' positions. Since there are '1's in the positions for 16 and 4, we need only add 16 plus 4 to arrive at 20 in our system. Got it? This is the same binary code used in computers.]

The Greek student smiles at that, and then fades and re-emerges wearing an Egyptian Robe and headdress—his face still the same. "I am Rathor, an initiate of Anhkaton's Egyptian mystery school. You can guess I have a very special opportunity to learn secrets revealed to very few people. Every week after completing my chores on my father's farm, I run up the steps to the Great Pyramid's entrance and am greeted by the Keeper, who then escorts me blindfolded into the very center of the pyramid into a chamber with a large sarcophagus, big enough to hold even a tall person like me. There we learn the truths of the Sun God Ra and the nature of being as well as the laws of the universe. Did you know even Pythagoras was here in his time? Eventually I hope to achieve my next initiation level. It is then that we get to lie in the sarcophagus and the high priest performs a special ceremony granting us magical abilities."

Abruptly Mr. Henderson reappears in recognizable form. "Much of humanity's progress, as you can see, happened over 3000 years ago and was making great progress up to about 300 A.D. when the Roman Empire collapsed from greed and pestilence; invaders marched into Europe and Egypt. Disease and famine became the norm. Let's hear from a young person living in the middle of that …".

To Mr. Henderson's left appears a young man dressed in a light tan blouse and brown puffy breeches. "I am Edward; I live in lands afar known as Britannia, later to be known as England. Yesterday my brother, baby sister and my dog Zig died of the plaque. Food is hard to come by and when we do get some it is often crawling with worms; foreigners are always invading and pillaging; governments are constantly fighting and changing leaders; kings and nobles are forever approaching us for taxes. We do have some fun, though; during holy-day festivities we get to watch the knights in colorful tights and heavy armor joust and play battle games and win prizes for the noble lady folk--It is a great jest!"

Edward goes 'Poof' and Mr. Henderson continues to instruct. "The Roman Christian Church seems to be in charge during this time span of 1000 years which you later call the Dark and Middle Ages. Few people in this time period remember the grandeur that was Rome or the freedom that was Greece."

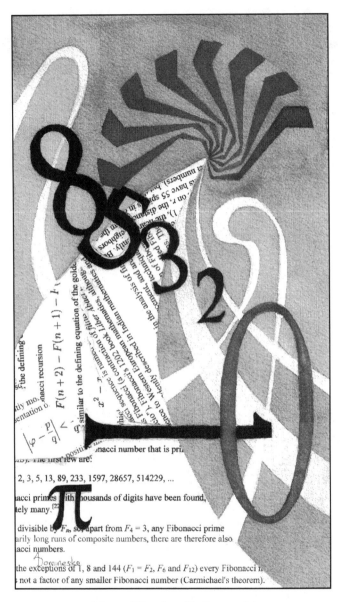

Magic of Numbers (A. Domineske)

"Ever since the prophet Jesus preached, converting many people to his belief system later named Christianity, the resulting Holy Roman Catholic Church had tried to help people through the dark times of disease and loss of ancient knowledge. Their religious monasteries were open to the needy and offered guidance to the townsfolk. The religious clerics or scribes copied books by hand for the nobility and priests; their detailed written records leave us to this day with a valuable recorded history."

"The church offered a moral balance between the rulers and the ruled; it was regarded as the authority of God's word, the Bible, and other holy works. As a result, the people depended upon the church for moral behavior, performance of baptismal, marriage, and other important rituals, as well as day to day ethical guidance. In time, unfortunately, the Church grew in power and started to manipulate the very people it was serving."

"The Church authorities felt it would be dangerous if the average person had ready access to the Bible because it was feared the people would interpret the teachings in their own way and that no one would agree on anything and the world would go into chaos. So when the printing press was invented and books were available to those who could afford it, the Church banned any translations of the Bible into a local language (especially those by other newly rising religious sects) and went so far as to execute those who spread such books—after all, they believed only a member of the true Church could translate the Latin Bible properly."

"As you can imagine, as people learned to read and write and underground groups distributed translations of the Bible, an ever increasing number of people were reading and interpreting the words of Jesus, thereby becoming self empowered. This ultimately led to a new level of human thinking and became the spark for a new rebirth of humanity called the Renaissance."

"So let's now travel to England in the 16th century and see what's going on. The English King Henry VIII popularly remembered for his six wives, recently died and his daughter Elizabeth from his second wife Anne Boleyn has the reign. She becomes known as Good Queen Bess."

"The reign of Henry VIII was especially important since it became the precursor to our present day form of democratic government. Henry created the concept of a Parliament-King where the King ruled with the approval of a group of prominent members of society known as Parliament. Today the Prime Minister rules England jointly with the British Parliament while America is served by an elected President supported by a Senate and House of Representatives."

"Queen Elizabeth and the nobility supported arts and higher education. Through her support, the arts (paintings and sculpture) flourished, theatres such as the Shakespearean Theatre became popular, and educational institutions including Oxford University were born. Likewise in Italy, small study groups, centered on Plato's philosophy, grew into the early colleges such as the Padua University where Galileo taught. At these universities new 'wizards' studied subjects such as Latin, Greek, geometry, rhetoric, economics, history, and astrology. Open discussions about the nature of love, logic and reason, cause and effect, justice and virtue were actually encouraged."

"This Renaissance (French for 'Rebirth') concept spread throughout Europe. It was re-focused on the ancient knowledge of the Greek, Roman and Egyptian Kingdoms emphasizing the value of individuals. This resulted in a new wave of thought and excitement that encouraged innovative thinking, individual rights, trade and an improved way of life. It was a time that encouraged the contributions of great minds such as Francis

Bacon, Renè Descartes, Thomas Hobbs, Blaise Pascal, Sir Isaac Newton and Galileo Galilei. Interestingly, soon after the doors of the mind opened, monarchies toppled, and republics thrived—for education always paves the way for improvement for everyone."

Mr. Henderson sits on a chair and continues: "Much of human life hasn't changed over several thousand years—families, eating habits, love, hate, war, money—always there, but in different forms. Yet some aspects of life have indeed changed, especially notable in the area of technology. Consider that only 100 years ago there were no cell phones, dial phones, cars, iPods®, iPads®, Droids®, televisions, computer games, Google, CDs, DVDs, chips, calculators, or computers."

"We all have heard the saying that 'history repeats itself'. Does this mean Mankind must repeat mistakes forever? Although it may seem that way, the answer is emphatically NO for two important reasons:

1. The youth today will learn about mankind's history well enough to apply the lessons learned and prevent it.

2. The dynamics of the vibration energy of today's world is actually changing as predicted by the great Wizards of history."

"The year 2012 stands for a momentous occasion of planetary and universal positioning which can happen only once every 36,000 years when our solar system crosses the center of its galaxy. It is believed beings born in our current time span (since 1987 approximately) have the new gift of being able to think in Quantum terms, can see the whole picture, and be aware of ALL the ramifications of a decision made (if you choose to develop this ability) rather than seeing things in a limited linear fashion. Some identify these groups as 'Indigo' Children."

"Hopefully this means you will not repeat the same mistakes because you realize what could possibly happen. This is the main reason you need to study history —learn what makes humans tick in many different historical scenarios such as the Roman Empire, Ancient Greece, the Dark Ages, the Renaissance, during famine, during prosperity, during wars, as well as the events of the modern world especially the story of the American Adventure. *As you connect to the past, you are creating the future.* As Wizards you will be able to create quickly with precision."

"The wizards of this world are the doers, those who make things happen. They know themselves so they can know humanity. What the future will actually be like is no longer guided by astrology but will be up to today's Wizards."

"Before concluding this class we will share with you a special magical number, called the *Golden Ratio.*"

The GOLDEN RATIO φ

Mr. Henderson is getting really excited as he talks about his favorite subject. "Although there are many, many magical features of numbers included in our ten digit system, we shall focus on a special set of whole numbers called the Fibonacci Series. This phenomenon shows up in so many facets of life on our planet and in the structure of our universe that it is a key component in the toolkit of the modern Wizard. You shall encounter its function in depth with Dr. Oiseau in Grotto 103."

"So let us begin to understand how it is created, so that we can later understand how to use it. There are many different series of numbers. For example 1, 2, 3, 4, 5 ... is a series of whole numbers from one to however large you can count. If you never stop counting, you will get close, but never reach the very last number called 'infinity' represented by the number 'eight' sleeping on its side— ∞.

Another series might be: 1, 3, 5, 7, 9, 11… a set of odd numbers on to ∞.

Or

The geometric series 1 + ½ + ¼ + ⅛ the total which never exceeds the value of 2

Or

For this study, the Fibonacci Series:

0, 1, 1, 2, 3, 5, 8, 13, 21, 34, 55, 89…

Can you see how it is created? It starts with nothing '0', followed with a something, a '1'. In other words, there was nothing in the universe, and then something was created. Then the '1' was given a companion '1'. The two ones combine into a duality '2', wherein everything in the universe exists having two natures. The '2' and '1' then combine to produce '3'. The '3' and the '2' combine to become '5'. Then '5' and '3' become '8'. And so on, *two adjacent numbers add up to create the next one.*

Can you do this forever? Yes. That defines the Fibonacci Series to infinity. You can even add, combine, square, divide, flip and rotate the Fibonacci numbers in many odd ways and still have a unique series. These properties are so unusual, it is *magical.*"

"These Fibonacci numbers 3, 5, 8, 13, 21, 34, 55, 89 show up in nature in various ways, such as in the petal arrangement of irises, marigolds, and daisies and in the limbs of elm, cherry, pear, and beech trees. The number of spirals on a pine cone (or pineapple) alternate in left and right rotation, usually in quantities of two consecutive Fibonacci numbers. These special relationships also show up in the web of the orb spider. In music, the black keys on a piano keyboard appear in groups of two and three within a set of eight white keys resulting in a total of thirteen per octave. Do these numbers look familiar? "

"Wait! There's more. If you calculate the *ratio* of any two consecutive numbers as the series grows, the ratio approaches the Magical number called the **Golden Ratio** commonly represented by the Greek character Phi - φ."

"Try it. Let's select '34' and '21'. '34' divided by '21' equals 1.6190, 55/34 is 1.6176, and 89/55 is 1.6182. Eventually, using ever larger numbers, you will get 1.6180. Actually calculated out to 31 decimals it becomes:

1.6180339887498948482045868343656

Even calculated out to 2000 decimals we find no repetition in the sequence of numbers. This is very unusual. A close approximation $(1+\sqrt{5})/2$ as determined on the Windows PC 'accessories' using its calculator's scientific option equals

1.6180339887498948482045868343656. This result is identical to at least thirty one decimal places.

Another interesting characteristic of φ is that it results exactly the same from the following trigonometric formula involving the dreaded number of the BEAST, ie 666: The sine of '666' plus the cosine of '6' times '6' times '6' (or cosine of '216') equals

-1.6180339887498948482045868343656"

Notice that it has the exact same digits as Phi but with a minus sign. Why? Because it is truly magical! Some reading this will say it only proves that it is a 'demonic' number, but they will get over it. Actually since the result was a minus, it might be construed as the shadow side of Phi, since all things in the universe have dual natures."

"Presentation of this number or any irrational number (one that cannot be expressed using whole numbers) would have banned one from Pythagoras' school because Pythagoras could not tolerate a universal truth represented with less than a whole number. I guess he had a time with Pi (3.1416), the ratio of the circle's diameter to the circumference, since it is NOT a whole number. (It is different from Phi in that after some point it is repetitive and it is not totally irrational since it can be represented as 22/7). Another famous irrational number, though, is 'e' or 2.7182818 ... very important in calculus."

"The Golden Ratio is critical to living matter; it shows up in the petals of a rose, the seeds of the apple, the formation of the nautilus shell, and the creation of the 5-pointed star or pentagram. It is everywhere in nature and therefore appears naturally aesthetic. The Nautilus shape is created by tracing Golden rectangles. A golden rectangle is one with the sides in proportion to the Golden Ratio. Observe the shape evolves out of the succession of golden rectangles below:

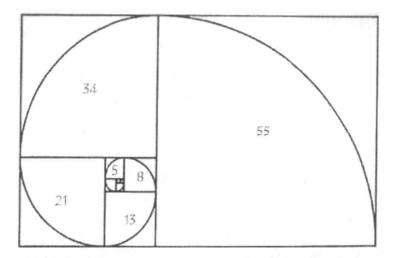

Our bodies grow in accordance with this ratio—look at the proportion of the bones of your fingers from the tips to the wrists and your legs from your toes to your hips, and the proportion of your body height to the height of your navel."

"Due to its naturally aesthetic proportions, it shows up in famous art including works of Dali, DaVinci, and Michaelangelo, as well as architectural structures including the Greek Parthenon, the Egyptian pyramid and the United Nations Building in New York City. Its pattern is studied by behavioral scientists and even shows up in the analysis of financial markets. As a tool, it is used by investors, musicians, healers and, well, Wizards."

"Can you not wonder in awe at the creation of man and nature as you study geometry and the nature of our numbering system? And this is only the beginning of the story. What other mysteries might be hidden in numbers? Hint: Look up Pascal's Triangle."

For the student earning money:

Another common feature of our number system is the capacity to compound and grow numbers. For example the number 1,000 doubled only 10 times becomes 1,024,000. Doubling is the same as compounding interest at 100%. Let's see, how many times would we have to grow at 50% to reach a million? It is about 17 times.

In our world, since 30% interest rate is common on credit cards, how many times would they have to charge you for your $1000 debt to grow to a million dollars? Would you believe less than 27 times?

Now reverse the thought and be conservative and ask how long would it take your savings of $1000 to grow at 20% interest <u>per month</u> to a million dollars? Answer: 38 months or about 3 years. Think about that. At the very low rate of 3% per month (if you could get it) it would take 20 years.

Time to think out of the box.

"With what you have learned, can you begin to grasp the potential of your future? Can you appreciate that 'knowledge will set you free'?" Socrates, the great philosopher and teacher of Plato said that first.

Are you ready to use magical powers for the good of mankind?

... And to perpetuate the expansion of consciousness so that you can

Be MORE Than You Can Be!

Carry the following thought as you travel through the Grottos:

Power comes to you when you have shown the universe that you understand the nuts and bolts of magic.

Knowledge is Power, Knowledge is Magic; Therefore, Magic is Power

Grotto 102:
Magic of Diversity

Sister Sulis emerges from the green puddle of water and shrieks in a high pitched cackle "Welcome, my dearies, to my world." She looks and acts like the witch from *Hansel & Gretel*. Did you expect otherwise? Suddenly with a wave of her hand (or is it a wand?), she transforms into her natural self: the wart disappears; her skin turns pink though with a slight greenish tint, and her hair becomes silky smooth—she is as beautiful as a woman can be.

A giant clear bubble appears slightly above; as it comes into focus, we can't help but look inside. Sister Sulis announces: "Today I share with you the workings of a typical modern gathering of Wiccans (male and female witches)."

In the bubble we see a typical married couple bustling around a 21st century kitchen. "Sam and Anita are the hosts for this month's Full Moon Circle. Anita, the coven's High Priestess is expecting up to 10 people from her coven tonight. Their home with a large fenced yard is ideal for a cool summer's eve ceremony."

Ding Dong. There goes the door bell. Anita wipes her hands, takes off her apron and asks Sam to get the door. Mary and Mike, the first couple to arrive, relax in the living room until all the guests arrive."

Ding Dong. Guests are arriving in a continuous stream as if all got off the same bus together. After some moments of chattering, Anita announces: "Welcome everyone, this evening our circle will be devoted to creating and sending healing energy. George's sister-in-law is scheduled for surgery next week and he has asked us to help. So, if you have anyone in mind who needs healing energy, write the person's name on a slip of paper and place it in this jar. Since it is so nice outside, we will do the circle in our backyard, if no one objects." As everyone nods OK, she reminds everyone, "We have extra robes in the closet if you need one". Some of guests don robes and Anita places a crown shaped as a half moon on her head. She leads the group outside and places a bouquet of flowers on a makeshift altar of glowing candles and ignites some sweet smelling incense. Amazingly, we can smell the aroma through the bubble.

Outside, under the moonlight, eleven people form a large circle, and the High Priestess walks around the outside of the circle clockwise three times scattering salt and water for cleansing while she repeats, "I draw this circle thrice about to keep all evil spirits out." The High Priestess completes the circle of 12 and with the congregation acclaims: "We bless and consecrate this circle with the elements air, fire, water, and earth in the name of our lady the Goddess and her consort, the horned God. So mote it be!"

From the East side of the circle, one of the members steps forward and says, "Blessed Be, beloved guardian of the East, Protect our circle." From the South side, another member steps out with, "As you come to us may you bring the warmth of the Sun. So mote it be!" From the West side, a third member says, "As you join us may you bring the cup of knowledge. So mote it be!" From the North side, a forth member says, "May you bring the strength of the mountains. So mote it be!"

The High Priestess then recites: "Blessed be thee, beloved God, warrior, hunter, provider, keeper of the fire. Be amongst us now." She lights a candle, rings a bell and follows with a recital of the Goddess, culminating in: "I am Maid and Moon and Mother. I am Crone tis well to learn. From my womb does all life issue. And to there it must return. So mote it be!"

Anita then addresses the group: "We hereby offer our intent to provide healing for those names and any others we might offer mentally", as she deposits the contents of the jar into the fire and returns to the circle, while the smoke carries their intentions into the ethers. As the congregation gathers their hands together, Anita leads a chant about Mother Earth. "Air I am, Fire I am, Water Earth and Spirit I am". As the rhythm builds up, they move in unison left and right with the music. As we watch, we feel the energy of their intent and excitement mount as they sing even louder and louder.... and then an abrupt silence is followed by clasped hands thrust upwards towards the sky while in unison they shout, "So Mote it Be!"

After a moment of silence, the High Priestess offers the ceremony of the wine and cakes: "As the athame is to the male, so is the chalice to the female." And with the congregation in unison: "Together they are one in truth. There is no greater 'magick' in the entire world than that of a man and woman joined together in love." Together they announce: "We thank you Goddess for the gifts of the land", while a member of the group passes cakes and wine to share. Then the High Priestess acclaims: "Beloved Goddess, beloved God, we thank you for your presence and protection. Go in Peace." She snuffs out the candles and removes her crown.

The four corner members acclaim: "Beloved guardian of the North, South, West, East, we thank you for your presence and protection. Go in Peace." The High Priestess walks around the circle counterclockwise and states, "The Rite is ended, go in Peace,

Blessed Be." The group returns to the home of Anita and Sam where they share a small feast.

The bubble slowly becomes opaque then disappears as Sister Sulis continues: "As you can surmise, the myths of 'evil' witches are not real. Our 'religion' is based on the power of nature and as a group we are called Wicca. Our belief system was popular in the world of the Celts (Ireland) long before the Romans brought in their Pagan beliefs that was later followed by Christianity. Pagans believed in gods and goddesses who behave much like humans. Later the newly created religions considered the Wiccans and Pagans as evil."

"In the Middle Ages little old ladies who gathered herbs and helped heal people's wounds and ailments were treated as evil witches and executed. Today pharmaceutical companies send scouts to the Amazon forests to gather herbs known by the native shamans (tribal healers) for analysis and then manufacture high priced drugs for sale at pharmacies and promote them to doctors for improved health."

"Now let's visit another ceremony, a popular one the world over." A new bubble about the size of an orange appears over Sister Sulis' head and quickly expands to a sizable bubble in which we see a small room with large doors, about two humans high. A young man pushes the swinging door open and enters into a vast almost cavern-like room with very high ceilings at least four humans high. As he enters we see him dipping his thumb and first two fingers into a dish of water, then touch his forehead, his chest, his left shoulder, his right shoulder, and then he follows other people towards an empty seat. As he enters a pew, he locates his seat, rests his knees on a soft cushion, and clasps his hands with fingertips pointing upward. Time accelerates in the bubble as we watch the young man stand, sit, kneel, stand, kneel, stand, sit … and finally we begin to hear voices …

As Sister Sulis slows time in the bubble, she says: "Listen!" The voices become distinguishable and we see a man in a white robe with what appears to be a violet sash across his shoulders down to the floor, an altar with lighted candles and incense burning behind him, and a golden cabinet housing a chalice of wine. Hanging above him we see a bronze statue of a man on a cross with nails in his hands and feet. "Let us pray. Remove our sins from us, O Lord. Through Christ our Lord, Amen."

The scene speeds up and we hear the priest leading the congregation with: "Kyrie, eleison, Kyrie, eleison, Kyrie, eleison." [Latin for "Lord, have mercy on us".]

The scene accelerates again and we hear: "Glory to God in the highest and on earth peace to men of good will. Let us Pray." After some readings from a holy book, we hear: "I believe in one God, the Father Almighty, Maker of heaven and earth, and of all things visible and invisible. And in one Lord, Jesus Christ, the only begotten Son of God, Born of the Father before all ages …"

As the congregation kneels, they say "And was made flesh by the Holy Spirit of the Virgin Mary and was made Man."

The scene accelerates to where the Priest holds up a white disk of flat bread called the 'host' while praying aloud: "Jesus says, 'take ye all and eat of this, for this is my body'. He then raises the chalice of wine and says: "take ye all and drink of this, for this is the chalice of my blood, of the new and eternal covenant …" After the Priest gives himself a host and drinks the wine, members of the congregation approach the altar, open their mouths and receive the 'Body and Blood of Jesus' from the Priest as he blesses each person. The service continues with a prayer: "Our Father, who art in heaven …" followed soon after with "Agnus Dei … Lamb of God, who take away the sins of the world, have mercy on us …" Soon we hear the dismissal as a statement and response:

"The Lord be with you. And with your spirit. Go the Mass is ended. Thanks be to God."

Upon hearing: "May almighty God bless you: the Father, the Son and the Holy Spirit. Amen", the congregation rises and returns to the entrance and exits while our bubble closes like an iris and Sister Sulis re-appears: "As you can see there are similarities between the Catholic service and the Wicca meeting; it was the practice of the early Church to adopt some of the local religious traditions of the people they were converting. The magical process of the 'communion' in the Catholic Church is uniquely considered the transubstantiation of the bread and wine *into* the body and blood of Jesus, whereas all other Christian rites consider it purely as symbolism."

"In the western world, the predominant belief system is Christianity; there are over 300 sects of non-Catholic Christianity based on the teachings of Jesus, all of which find one or more elements of the Catholic Church incongruous with their personal calling. Some are more political then others. Some focus on Jesus the man; some focus on Saints and holidays. Some are based on biblical prophecies and emphasize the next coming and others focus on local humanitarian deeds or local community support. All, however, emphasize some aspect of Jesus' teachings.

There are Christian-like groups that are not represented by a leader and often without a doctrine such as the Unitarian Universalists, the Mennonites, and the Quakers. The UU accommodates all religious groups including Wicca and pagans, the Mennonites have a holistic approach, and the Quaker Meeting is based on individual inward authority—the idea that each person expresses the creator as an inner light rather than rely on an outward authority for direction, such as a Pope or Priest or some designated leader of the belief system.

In the East the more prominent belief systems include Hindi, Islam, Judaism, Buddhism, and Taoism, all different yet all the same. In all religions there are secret sects of greater knowledge such as the Sufis (Islam), the Essenes (Judaism), Christian Mystics, Sikhs (Hindi), and other Avatars. Alternatively, throughout history, there were always special orders, secret societies, and private groups who kept alive the Universal truths known by the early Wiccans, Wizards, and pre-Church Christians.

Sister Sulis then directs our attention: "Look in this expanding bubble on my right. Whom do you recognize?" Looking at the party under the Willow Tree, we see a group of prophets, avatars, shamans, medicine men, yogis, mystics, and teachers. These include Jesus, Siddhartha Gautama (Buddha), Isaac from Abraham, Ishmael from Abraham, Muhammad, Moses, Krishna, and Zoroaster as well as the less familiar Martin Luther, John Calvin, Joseph Smith, Brigham Young, John Smyth, Mary Baker Eddy, Aimee Semple McPherson, Charles Taze Russell, Menno Simons, Guru Nanak, John Wesley, several Dalai Lamas, Mother Theresa, Gandhi, Merlyn, and many more.

"Some groups have no physical leaders such as the American Indian. Yet the American Indian has to this day, a profound understanding of humanity's connection with the Great Spirit. They see the sacred in <u>all</u> of the natural world, seen and unseen. They believe all humans, regardless of their beliefs, are imbued with a part of the Spirit, the Creator. They never understood 'white' man's over zealous fearful reaction to their natural ways."

"Although all of these representatives presented divine messages appropriate for their period, many of their messages continue to inspire us today. Most religions using churches, synagogues, or mosques are designed for members to get together to share a common understanding of their relationship to a creator, God, Supreme Being, All knowing, or Universal consciousness; to praise him or her, seek guidance, and to help each other in religious and community manners."

"Some of these beliefs divided the world into heaven and hell while some deny the existence of hell. Some define appropriate and inappropriate behavior as the written holy word and some consider right or wrong as simply what is good or harmful to the continuation of the human race. Some focus on an imagined end of the world while others focus on the here and now. Some fear the wrath of an anthropomorphic god and others revel in the light of the infinite spirit. And so the variety goes …"

"We are all in the same flying boat, the planet earth known as Gaia, and we are all trying to live our lives to some standard. We can only choose a belief system that is most comfortable for ourselves; often it is the one we grew up with. We <u>must</u>, however, choose to live together and <u>respect</u> each other's belief systems if we are to survive."

"In the spirit world we all work together to help mankind. We offer you moral codes and guidance in how to live. The spirit world presents each culture with a religious variant that makes sense to that culture. There is no right or wrong belief system. The importance is not in <u>what</u> we believe but in <u>how</u> we believe. Socrates in his time stated '***Know Thyself***'. In learning about ourselves we learn about our creator and in learning about our creator we learn about ourselves."

Sister Sulis suddenly expands to twice her size, like a Xerox copy and declares: "It is time to address the issue of Black Magic since it arises when the word 'magic' is mentioned. In our Western culture, wizards are often shown as powerful men while witches are depicted as evil women. Let's be quite clear on this. ALL people, men and women, can be both evil and good whether they practice magic or not, or pray or not, or speak thoughts or not. Whenever anyone has a 'bad' intent or purpose, they are performing Black Magic to some degree especially if they direct their thoughts onto someone else maliciously. As Dr. Oiseau will make quite clear in Grotto 103, the human with evil intentions creates havoc and serious damage more to themselves than to others. If negative intents arise in your mind, it is best to discard them or re-arrange them into positive intents."

Under the Willow Tree; Magic of Diversity (A. Domineske.)

"Eastern philosophies teach evil as a shadow or lack of light. The whole devil and 'witches' concept is a construct of later western philosophies. It is true that some humans take advantage of religions and use it to manipulate and control their fellow humans. But it is the Wise and those educated in the ways of the Wizard who keep things in balance."

Sister Sulis reduces to her normal size and says: "Our goal in this Grotto is to show you the interdependence of humanity. You saw how man has created many, many systems of worship and acknowledgement of a Creator. For the balance of this Grotto we will show you other evidence that we are all truly of one source and that the differences among humans is only one of perception."

The DNA Factor

"A recent global geno-graphic project sponsored by the National Geographic Society and published in their magazine March, 2006 focused on gathering and analyzing the DNA of a large population of individuals of varying cultures and ethnic races. This scientific study confirms that ***ALL the variously shaped and shaded people of Earth trace their ancestry to African roots*** some 150,000 years ago. In fact the study shows that the migratory paths across the globe started in Africa and spread to all continents. Through genetically selective chromosomes, people adapted a color and other ethnic features suitable to their adopted climate and environment resulting in the many cultural differences of today."

"The realization that we are all truly brothers and sisters borne of the planet Gaia is the <u>seed</u> of the now developing ***paradigm shift of human consciousness***. It is evident in the increased social interest in ecology—the new Green, rising socially responsible businesses, alternative healing techniques, emphasis on wellness care and preventative medicine, a renewed focus on organic farming, and an expanded interest in the ways of the Wizard. We are changing from a society of self-interest to one with a shared spiritual consciousness. Globalization is not just economics; it encompasses the spirit of man in all its variations."

Sister Sulis pauses, allowing us to absorb all this, then solicits our attention, "Now, relax and enjoy this story about Tamil, a monkey in the Amazon and how his culture changed."

A bubble—Sister Sulis' favorite manifesting tool—appears and this time we actually enter it and float over a jungle. In the distance we see a UPS cargo plane in trouble. As smoke spews out of one of its four engines, the navigator calls for help on his radio, "May Day, May Day, UPS 102 is going down, our coordinates are … ." Then Captain Iqbal, an Indian pilot and Sikh, evident by the UPS-brown turban on his head, announces, "Not so fast, I think we can recover if we drop some cargo quickly. Here goes!"

He pushes a button and the cargo doors open, dropping several large crates, while the plane gains some altitude. "Well, I think that did it, we are going to just clear the trees. Alert the nearest landing strip that we are coming down for repair." Luke Skyfall, the navigator, voiced in a tone of relief, "Thank God. I guess Apple will not deliver their load of 10,000 iPhones® on this trip! I suppose their insurance will cover it." As the plane soars off in the distance the crates explode open while falling, distributing iPhones® over the jungle for many miles.

Our view is now at the jungle floor focused on a very smart monkey named Tamil. Tamil is resting on the trunk of a large tree, playing with an iPhone®, though he does not know what it is. The quizzical look on his face reveals he is not sure what to make of it; he turns it this way and turns it that way and he turns it every which way. He jumps up and down, both excited and frustrated with more turning and flipping in his hands. After several minutes he accidentally hits a button and turns it one more time, and to his shock and amazement he sees a monkey's face on it. "Wait, that's no ordinary monkey", he thinks, as he studies the face's expression. "It is Tamil. It is me. How did I get in there? I am here." Further playing around, he connects the dots and discovers that pressing a certain spot on the device displays whatever he is pointing the iPhone® at. Running around in circles, he can't wait to show this to his brothers. "Wait until they see what I found."

He sees his family sitting in a distant grove; they seem to be intent on some prey. On closer scrutiny, Tamil sees they are examining a device similar to his. "Hey guys", he says in monkey lingo, as he sees them struggle with trying to figure out what it is, expands his chest in pride, "I know what that is and how to make it do something."

Well, after that everyone looked up to Tamil, for he knew something no one else knew. Before long, he taught his whole clan how to get images into the device. The next day they visited their cousins from another clan in another valley. To Tamil's surprise everyone there had these 'iPhones®' too. "Where did you get those?" Tamil asked cautiously. "Oh, they fell from the gods above, they must be meant for us, but we can't figure out what it means."

Soon Tamil became the guru of the iPhone® and everyone was running around taking pictures. This went on for several days and Tamil decided he would visit another clan.

Tamil's Adventure (A. Domineske)

Pretty soon he had trained 100 monkeys on how to use the magical gift from heaven. He was getting rich on bananas! Tamil decided it was time to travel to a distant grove and visit the Big Tribe many tree swings away. He brought one of his cousins to help carry the bananas he will collect.

To his surprise, when he arrived, every monkey already had an iPhone®. So he went up to one and said, "Hey, I can teach you how to use those." The Big Monkey looked at him and said, "We already know how to use it, look here's your picture," as he snaps it in Tamil's face.

Needless to say, Tamil was a bit despondent at that, but then an idea clicked in his head. "I know! I will teach their young pups and their elders how to do it." Well, as he visited the members of the community, he found the knowledge had already passed through generations of monkeys. It seems the knowledge and abilities were traveling faster than he could imagine. And truth be told, all generations of monkeys after that seemed to be born with that wisdom. Well, of course Tamil returned home, sad and banana-less.

"So how did they all learn to use the iPhone®. without Tamil's teaching? The world famous biologist Rupert Sheldrake termed the phenomena, the '100th Monkey Theory'. I thought he should have named it 'Tamil's Gift'", joked Sister Sulis. "Due to what Sheldrake termed the Morphic Field, the knowledge was transmitted through time and space to all the monkeys after the number of monkeys who learned it reached some critical mass--in this case 100 monkeys."

"Of course, this is a silly story, but it demonstrates the theory of *morphic resonance*. Professor Gustaf and Dr. Oiseau will clarify this process and demonstrate its value to the Wizard. Today it is believed that if but <u>one tenth of one percent</u> of the human population embrace a concept such as Universal Love, it will permeate everyone, everywhere. Isn't that a wonderful thought?"

Sister Sulis pulls us out of the bubble and offers, "For more fun, I will now share with you a colorful adventure, an adventure into the world of divination, an idea common to many Witches and Wizards." This time Sister Sulis displays a panorama screen around the stage as we watch the visions from all angles.

"Astrology is one of the oldest sciences of man, dating before the Babylonia period, well before written records. It reflects an early understanding of the cosmos and man's place in it. Used by the ancient cities of Greece and the kingdoms of Egypt, it was often the predictor of the success and failures of battles and other major events. Today it is most useful in identifying the strengths and weaknesses of individuals to guide them on their journey through life. Based on the positions of the planets within the background of stars, the calculation methodology of the charts has not changed over thousands of years."

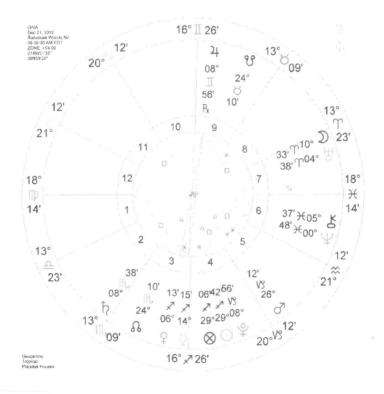

Chart of Gaia, 12/21/2012; ©1994 Matrix Software, Big Rapids, MI

"Above is a typical astrological chart. It consists of an inner ring with numbers representing the twelve divisions called 'houses' or affairs of man including the ego (first house), money, communication, home, children, health, partnerships, death, beliefs, vocation, hope, and the subconscious (12th house). The entry and exit of each house is marked on the wheel's outer ring with the sign of the constellation—the backdrop of the planets position and the specific degree within it (each has a 30 degree movement within a circle of 360 degrees). Planets are positioned on the chart based on their location in the heavens and thence fall within specific houses indicating their effects upon specific human issues."

"In the very center of the circle are lines connecting planets which have angular relationships of 0 (zero) known as conjunct, 60 degrees known as sextile, 90 degrees known as square, 120 degrees known as trine, and 180 degrees known as oppositions."

"Astrology is the interpretation of the effects of the planets in our solar system against a backdrop of stars grouped into constellations within our galaxy upon our planet Gaia and her inhabitants—guess who? This specific chart represents a specific date, time and location—in this case December 21, 2012 in NJ, USA at midnight. Although the Ancient Mayans predicted this date by ending their calendar on that moment, our science community recently discovered that our galaxy will cross the center of the universe on that specific date, a phenomenon that can only happen every 36,000 years."

"Astrological charts can be constructed very accurately because the data is based on actual astronomical and mathematical records. Besides the astronomical knowledge, the tradition of the interpretation has also been carried down through the centuries.

The experienced astrologer will read the chart by noting the position of the planets and their relationship to each other, add a pinch of intuitive judgment, and produce a thorough analysis of the person or subject being studied based upon a date of significance such as one's birthday or origin date."

"Concurrent with this technology, we find that other methods of divination were developed in the East. The Chinese created the I-Ching Book of Wisdom consisting of 64 hexagrams or patterns. The Indian Yogis offered us the 7 point Chakra System of energy centers within the human body. Modern science offers the double Helix DNA genetic pattern."

Combining all these modalities (astrology, I-Ching, and Chakras) with the Jewish Kabbalah, and modern DNA genetics, results in the ***Human Design System*** as channeled to Canadian Robert Alan Krakower in 1987 over an eight day period. Although a skeptic, he embraced the system, adopted the name Ra Uru Hu and presented it to the world in 1992. The Human Design System is the first new pattern of mankind since Astrology and integrates the various bodies of knowledge known to man at this time. It is an integration of cultures and paves the way for the paradigm shift we are all beginning to feel. In addition it makes for a very colorful display (see the website identified in the Crypt for the color version).

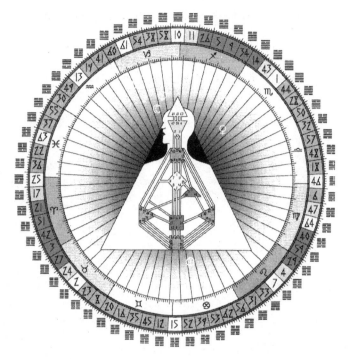

*Rave Mandalla™ and the Rave Body Graph™ are
registered trademarks of Jovian Archive Media*

"Above is the Human Design Mandalla™ including the Human Rave™ chart within an astrological framework. This wonderful tool displays each individual's unique imprint or pattern as programmed upon birth <u>and</u> conception. The inner ring consists of the 12 constellations in counter-clockwise order starting at '9 o'clock'. The outer ring displays the 64 hexagrams of the I-Ching Book of Wisdom. The middle ring is a fixed assignment of 64 numbered gates, one for each hexagram. The individual's planet positions as defined from astrological calculations are placed within the Mandalla™ in line with a specific gate (not shown in this mandalla)."

"Relationships among the gates is then displayed within the center of the Mandalla on what is known as the Human Rave™ containing nine energy centers (the seven chakras plus two more). Each center is home to specific gates; gates are opened when a planet is positioned in the gate. Then two open gates on a channel become colored either red or black. (None are connected in this graphic). This is where the Human Design Practitioner (HDP) takes over and studies the channels among the chakra centers for activities from both the personality view (based on birth time) and the human design view (based on conception time). It is used as a tool to assist us in aligning with our probable destinies and encourage us to be masters of our destinies."

Sister Sulis concludes: "I hope you enjoyed your visit to my Grotto. You have completed round Two of the circuit of Grottos on the way to the Quantum Completion. I trust that with Mr. Henderson's help, we have excited the wizard in you to embrace diversity while you expand your knowledge exploring Dr. Oiseau's and Professor Gustaf's Grottos. So here are my closing thoughts on being a Wizard."

"The true Wizard is one who understands his/her world in its many manifestations, wields control of his own life, and takes one's responsibilities seriously including abiding to the ethics of one's soul, always being true to oneself and striving to grow in line with one's highest calling. Remember, the Wizard uses internal power techniques to achieve goals in line with the laws of nature and focuses magical intent for the overall good."

As a two foot round mirror appears before each of us, Sister Sulis proclaims, "Let us now look into the magic mirror of wisdom as you re-affirm your intent to be more than you can be". This magical scrying mirror is one rarely seen; it has no apparent reflection yet you can see deep within it.

The Magical Mirror

"Now as you gaze into the 'Mirror of Wisdom', see and <u>merge</u> yourself among the Wizards of the Modern World—who are daily impacting the world you live in--including such personalities as Jean Houston, Depak Chopra, Gregg Braden, Louise Hay, Eckhart Tolle, Carolyn Myss, Jan Tober, Lee Carroll, Dalai Lama, and many, many, more …

Grotto 103:
The Magic of Life

As our class of twelve enters Grotto 103, we are surprised to find ourselves in a large cave the size of a city, the roof a sky of blue pastels and walls too far away even to discern. Other groups of twelve are floating in the distance. This must be the largest classroom ever. Hanging in air in 3D fashion are two people, a male and a female, both with long hair yet differentiated by the large shoulders of the male and the shapely figure of a female.

As we watch the amazing view in front of us, Dr. Oiseau flies into the scene; yes, flies, she is part bird you know. (Incidentally, 'Oiseau' is French for bird.) Actually at the moment she looks like a beautiful Blue Heron—a rather large bird with expansive wings and long beak.

Dr. Oiseau also known as Robyn (why her name is not Heron we have no clue) explains, "Observe, my novice Wizards, what I am about to reveal to you." She waves her open wings over our eyes and suddenly the two flesh and blood persons are encased in two large vibrant eggs of various colored spheres. Instead of the usual body parts we see a column of colored balls of light, seven balls to be exact, each a different color of the rainbow from violet at the top of the head to red at the bottom of the spine. The two humans haven't really changed; only they do seem different. Other than the balls of energy we are aware of strings of white light flowing through their bodies from their heads down to their toes and fingertips.

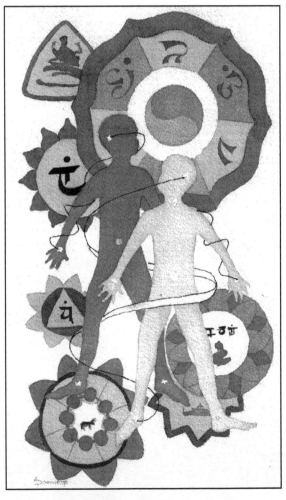

MAGIC OF BEING (A. Domineske)

"What you are seeing is the human energy form consisting of the Indian Chakra System of seven major energy centers combined with the Chinese Meridian System. Each vortex of concentrated energy is associated with various body parts, each with a Sanskrit name (ancient language of India, the precursor to the Indo-European languages from which English is derived), an associated color (as in the rainbow), and an Astrological ruling planet."

"The seven chakras are, starting from the base of the spine, the RED Root Chakra, the ORANGE Sacral Chakra located near the navel, (also known by the Chinese as the Dan Tien), the YELLOW Solar Plexus located between the chest bone and navel, the GREEN Heart Chakra near the Heart, the BLUE Throat Chakra where one would expect it, the INDIGO Third Eye Chakra on the forehead, and finally the White or VIOLET Crown Chakra (yes, you guessed it) on the top of the Head."

"You are seeing the true nature of the human; humans are not merely a conglomeration of body parts but are spiritual beings of light vibrations that manifest to our sense of sight as heart, lungs, skin and bones. Excuse me," as she returns to her female shape in a pastel blue dress and continues, "The chakras are our main energy centers, the Chinese meridians are the internal pathways for this flowing energy called Chi."

"So how does this knowledge serve us? Let me explain. Suppose you have a painful sore throat. With western medicine you would attend a medical practitioner such as a doctor who would look at your throat and search for infections or germs and then offer a prescription for some medicine that would 'kill' microbes or ease the pain."

"The shaman or spiritual healer, on the other hand, might intone sounds over your body, place crystals over the vortex centers, and use his hands to 'massage' the energy fields to promote self healing."

"The Eastern practitioner would study your pulse (actually there are two pulse patterns), examine your tongue, listen to your symptoms and identify a particular imbalance in your body followed with a recommendation of Herbs, acupuncture, or acupressure. Acupuncture uses fine stainless needles while acupressure treatments employ physical pressure; both release trapped energy by removing blockages and allow the flow of Chi—the life force, to expedite healing." (Author's note: Chi is sometimes spelled Qi; it is known as *Prana* in the Indian tradition.

"So as a Wizard what would you do? First you practice what you are already trained to do. Then you apply other wisdom concepts such as the Eastern methodologies to expedite the healing process. For example, you first visit your doctor who will analyze your symptoms and recommend ways to treat it. Then you analyze the source of the issue from the point of view of energy. An imbalance in the throat infers that the throat chakra and its associated meridians are out of balance. You might notice intense energy in the form of heat in the neck and you might ask yourself what is going on in your life regarding the process of speaking or expressing yourself (items governed by this area). What habitual thinking are you stuck in? What might be the root cause of the problem energetically? At this point you might decide to seek a practitioner who specializes in Eastern medicine, or you might apply some of the techniques the Headmaster will outline."

"As you can guess, an imbalance in your energy will often manifest in physical ways, including illness, obesity, poor self-image, weak energy, or even damaged organs in severe cases. As a Wizard, you want these energy centers to be at their optimum, fully functional, and glowing with power. The Eastern healing techniques are methods of energy alignment dealing with the root causes; Western techniques focus on identifying physical causes and re-arranging or repairing the body's cells with chemistry or physical therapy. It is best to combine both the Eastern and Western techniques for an effective well being."

"My goal", Dr. Robyn says "is to help you be in perfect harmony with your life force so that the manifestation of your physical body is at its optimum and that you can function effectively as a Wizard."

"Before we delve into the nature of vibration and energy that you are, we shall approach the concept of health and welfare you are most comfortable with—the old standard—sleep, exercise and a balanced diet—but in the terms of energy balance, or the Taoist Yin and Yang of it. The traditional symbol for balance is the circle split into two parts—the Yin and the Yang. Notice the small circles indicating there is some Yang in Yin and some Yin in Yang."

YIN/YANG

"Taoism believes in the balance of nature where all things, matter and energy, have two natures—a masculine and a feminine, an up and a down, a push and a pull, a black and white, a yin and a yang. Life is a pulsating energy moving forward and backward— an ebb and flow. A healthy being is a balanced being, reflecting equality in both natures. So in the realm of nourishing our bodies with good eating habits, the rule is to eat in moderation while balancing the Yin and Yang foods. Eating too many hamburgers is simply too much Yang and needs to be balanced with Yin foods such as vegetables. How do you know if you have too much Yang or too much Yin? Are you gaining too much weight? Do you feel sluggish and tired too often? Are you having problems learning new things? Are you unsuccessful in getting what you want, i.e. attracting the energy, people, and money that you want in your life? Well, then, you probably are not in balance."

"Of greatest concern to us in your current state of energy is your general lack of exercise; and I don't mean push ups and sit-ups; I mean a healthy use of your muscles and bones and tendons. Like any machine, non-use will result in 'rust' and a permanent breakdown. From an energy standpoint, you want the pathways open to encourage the efficient flow of energy throughout your body. Your body is a support system for your mind, not the other way around."

"During the agricultural ages of man, physical exercise was a natural event in the process of growing food, tilling the fields and surviving. Today, your body sits in moving vehicles and works within confined areas rarely having the opportunity of developing muscles and maintaining a healthy energy flow. In your younger years, you are more naturally active but as you get older, the opportunities for an active lifestyle diminish. Having a game of baseball with your friends, for example, is not likely when you are juggling the duties involved with a family, children and a job. It is good practice to focus more on 'one on one' sport activities such as dance, bowling, badminton, tennis, racquet ball or even single activities such as yoga, gymnastics, swimming, martial arts, and tai chi or even working out in a gym. All these you can do with a friend or partner on a regular basis and at any age. The key is to find something you enjoy and then create a good habit that will serve you in subsequent years."

"A few words about Tai Chi because it is most conducive for the developing Wizard throughout one's entire life. Tai Chi is an ancient exercise/dance form that helps you develop an inner peace combined with an outward strength. The meridian lines of force you saw in the human body earlier are the pathways of energy; health is best when these pathways are clear and Chi can flow freely. The Tai Chi student learns to open the pathways allowing the life force to flow and maintain all parts of the body in a healthy and alive condition. The student learns the intricacy of the Yin and Yang principles of balance while learning the movements of Tai Chi. To the observer, Tai Chi moves slowly and therefore appears easy; it is not difficult to learn but requires a focus of the mind on the body and its internal energy. The more you can relax the outer mind, the greater the outward force. You can appreciate why the best martial artists of Karate, Jujitsu, Kendo, and Aikido incorporate the principles of Tai Chi into their arts. Tai Chi also has a martial arts component called Baqua that takes advantage of the opponent's energy without consuming one's own energy. Now, how cool is that?" (Check out the Crypt for more information about Tai Chi.)

"Rest or sleep is also an important ingredient in life. *Science News* recently reported that for the young, quality of sleep is important, while for the elder, quantity of sleep is important.

Make sure you have adequate sleep so your performance in all you do is top notch. How we appear physically is a reflection of our energy pattern; and our energy pattern is a <u>direct result of our thinking</u>. So be aware of negative habitual thinking. Not only does negative thought create energy blockages, it promotes bad habits not to your best interest. In our normal growth process we create <u>both</u> negative and positive patterns of habitual thinking. Thought patterns you acquired in stressful situations may not do you justice now. For example, you might have had a frightening encounter with a dog at age three and now when approached by a dog you automatically respond with the habitual thought 'I must avoid you, you are not good for me'. This kind of habitual thought response based upon a deeply submerged memory in your subconscious can be resolved during the process of *healing* otherwise known as 'energy <u>balancing</u>'. It is a good idea to free yourself of such subject-object thinking so you are able to think outside the box."

"A recent process developed by the British kinesiologist Andrew Kemp uses frequencies of sound and color combined with our recent acquaintance the **Fibonacci Series** to provide healing energy to our physical, mental, emotional and spiritual bodies. Kinesiology is based on the body intelligence (DNA) inherent in every living cell. By stimulating our body's natural healing powers with direct cellular instructions through the written word, numbers, fractal equations, sound, color, and symbols, we achieve a balance of our energy system."

"Andrew Kemp's primary 'code' as used in his Quantum K process is based on Fibonacci numbers and fractal geometry. (A Fractal is a mathematical construct or a fragmented geometric shape that can be split into identical shapes much like a hologram.) The twelve number sequences (again with the number *twelve*) communicate directly with our DNA, stimulating these basic building blocks of life to release negative programming and to rebuild using a positive set of instructions. The fractal equations provide the blueprint for our DNA to follow. Fractals define the structure of all living things—cells, plants, mountains and planets; they are particularly applicable to the structure and proportions of the human body—in line with the Golden Ratio."

"Here is a written sample of the work from Mr. Kemp's published work, *Quantum K*. (Free on his website; see the Crypt for references.)

Notice the reference to Fibonacci sequence, sound notes, octaves, colors, stones, plants, and harmonics. References to flower essences, herbs, and crystals all add to the communication with the body intelligence. Each Quantum K healing process involves thought transference to your being at conscious and unconscious levels. Mr. Kemp's free 23 minute process is available to anyone who can access the Internet. It is an excellent practice for all Wizards."

- ***Restore DNA helixes to their highest potential.***

  Fibonacci Sequence: $F(n+2) = F(n+1) + F(n)- +3$ dimensions Blue

  B,F,G Major Octaves C2,3,4,5 and 6. Starting (n) = 1 and (n+1) = 2

  Crystal: Emerald

  Plant: Sandalwood

  Master number 11

  Number 2 4 5 6 7 9 2 3 4 6 8 9

  Gateway 8 1 1 1 1 0 1 0 1 1 1 0 0

- *Remove all emotional blocks that inhibit the communication between our DNA and the crystalline lattice around it.*

Crystal: Ulexite Plant: Clove

Master number 7

Number 1 6 8 3 1 9 1 8 3 7 2 3

Gateway 9 0 0 0 0 0 0 0 1 1 1 0

"These two examples refer to the human DNA and the crystalline lattice. As you studied in the Rave Chart in Grotto 2 and the Chakra system in this Grotto, the energy field around each human known as the crystalline lattice is also surrounding each individual's unique energy pattern defined in his DNA genetic code. Since we are immersed in the universe's lattice, all DNA is interconnected regardless of time or space. This means there is a direct link between each and every human on the planet."

As transmitted by Kryon through Lee Carroll:

"The elegance of DNA is far beyond your comprehension. It contains the history of the Universe, of you, and of the primary issues of your being. It is responsive to your thoughts and actions, and waits patiently for activation. It is the core interactive architectural structure of life in the universe, and is profoundly spiritual."

(See the Crypt for further information)

Dr. Robyn now appears more down to earth standing on her two feet in her white feathery medical robe, "Now is a good time to pause and absorb what we have presented so far. Please take a moment and reflect on how you want to present your physical self to the world."

* * *

"For our next phase of this Grotto and in preparation of a better understanding of '*thought*', I have invited Professor Gustaf von Lichtenstein to present an explanation of energy or 'vibrations' as it is commonly called. So, please give him your full attention; the subject of vibration is the key to understanding the Power of your thought."

Meanwhile the doctor changes to a small hummingbird and hovers in a watchful gaze over the stage. Professor Gustaf comes onto the stage in full regalia with a flowing robe of rainbow colors, wearing a funny top hat radiating lightning sparks, a staff with a silver ball in his right hand, and a bunch of green rubber bands in his left hand. "Aha, I see that I have your attention. I hope you have enjoyed Sister Sulis' and Dr. Oiseau's dramatic performances so far. Robyn invited me to explain the topic of vibrations and I most graciously accepted." He bows down in the oriental fashion of respect, his beard pointing to the floor.

"So let us begin!" he exclaims as he hands out a broken rubber band to each student. "Now, each of you has a rubber string. Hold the ends apart and grab the middle with your third hand." He suddenly remembers that humans have only two hands. "Oops, wrong group. You will have to hold one end in your teeth and use your free hand to pull the rubber band from the center. Pull it far enough to stretch it so that when you let it loose it makes a twang sound."

"As it moves back and forth it is *vibrating*. Each complete movement is one vibration or cycle. Of course, it vibrates so fast, it is hard to count them. This is how the strings of a guitar, violin, or piano work. The string moves rapidly back and forth compressing the air while your ear drums sense the change in air pressure and your brain interprets it all as sound. Our ears are designed to be sensitive to a wide range of vibrations through the air from deep low bass sounds to very high pitched piercing noises; if there were no air you would hear absolutely nothing."

"The speed of the movement or frequency is measured in cycles per second. Scientists now call this measurement the Hertz, named after Heinrich Rudolf Hertz, a late 1800 German Physicist who demonstrated the existence of electromagnetic waves. The larger the number, the higher the frequency, the higher the musical note emitted by the movement of the string. So a low 'C' note originates from a vibration of 16 hertz or 16 cycles per second. The high 'C' note on the piano vibrates at 8192 hertz. The human ear might hear up to 20,000 hertz depending upon whose head the ears are attached to. Man's best friend, the canine, can hear up to 60,000 hertz."

"The piano keyboard has 8 'C' notes between the low 'C' and the high 'C'. Each of the 8 'C' notes is an octave apart. An octave is an exact double; so you will find 'C' notes at these frequencies: 32, 64, 128, 256, 512, 1024, 2048, and 4096 hertz as well as the forementioned 16 and 8192 hertz."

[Author's note: Follow this train of thought because the potential of its power is *profound*.]

"Pythagoras had fun exploring the nature of music. He discovered that two notes an octave apart would resonate together. He noticed that a wire struck in the middle would not only vibrate in the middle but in the middles of each of their halves, and their halves and so on. He was amazed that creating a vibration of 256 hertz, for example, actually results in sounds at many octaves above the original, although the sound strengths further out were somewhat weaker and could barely be heard."

"Have you ever listened to music you could actually feel? Vibrations below 16 hertz are in the realm of *feeling* or the sense of touch. Then what happens above 20,000 hertz? Well, it might be heard by some creatures such as dogs, but generally at some point a vibration frequency no longer shows up as sound but as something else. In the range of 60,000 hertz to 500 Million hertz we find electromagnetic waves, generated by magnetic and electrical impulses either naturally from space or from radio devices. Because these numbers are so large, we refer to them by their octaves. Above the 28th octave are 10 octaves of frequencies called microwaves, one of which is in your microwave oven. Another 10 octaves higher are infrared waves, commonly known as heat. Finally in the 49th or 50th octave is the phenomenon of light energy—the only octave of energy we can 'see'."

"Now things get really interesting. Of the entire spectrum of known vibrations, only a very small 2 octave range is visible light, consisting of colors starting at the lowest frequency with red, followed by orange, yellow, green, blue and violet at the high end with infinite shades in between. This is the portion of frequencies that humans perceive in their daily life. And it is no accident this is the same order of colors you see in the rainbow as Red, Orange, Yellow, Green, Blue, and Violet (ROYGBV)."

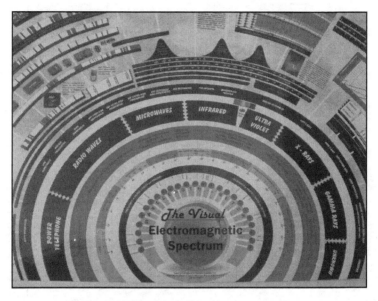

VIBRATIONS Visual Electromagnetic Spectrum,
Hubbard Scientific © 2010, P/N 4100

"Due to the unwieldy nature of large numbers such as 1,000,000,000,000,000 hertz, these are presented in abbreviated format, or in this case, 1000 terahertz where *tera* represents 12 zeros. The visible spectrum of color, therefore, is in the range of 430 to 750 terahertz. Colored light however is often measured as the width of its energy cycle in Ångstrom units. The higher the frequency the shorter the distance between pulses, hence the range of its width varies from 7000 Ångstrom to 4000 Ångstroms from the lowest frequency to the higher frequency."

"Ok, so how does energy with speeds beyond light show up? First is the familiar ultraviolet light in the 51st to 56th octaves followed by the x-ray in the 57th to 62nd octaves, an energy most familiar to hospital technicians. Current discoveries in science are only beginning to hint at what lies beyond that, beyond even gamma and cosmic rays received from space. Science defines octaves beyond 80 as *Unknown*. Mystics have always proclaimed that the very high frequencies represent the universal life force and possibly even the Soul—something to think about when you attend the next Grotto."

"Just as octaves of sound played together resonate well, octaves across the different bands of frequency types can resonate with interesting effects. For example, a 'G' note at 3840 hertz, in the 12th octave sound band produces a resonant frequency in the 24th octave at 15,728,640 hertz in the radio wave range while also resonating with a yellowish color in the 49th octave at 527,765,581,332,482 hertz, or 527 Terahertz or at a wavelength of 5710 Angstroms. Hence the 'G' note resonates with a shade of yellow."

"Can you grasp the significance of this as serious potential for the Wizard? How focusing on something easy like a color can result in effects to the body at the frequencies of the chakras? We are constantly resonating through the entire spectrum of energy from the familiar vibrations of sound and color to areas yet only imagined by science."

"Please take a moment to think about this phenomenon as it holds the key to the magic process."

"Now is a good time to return you to Dr. Oiseau who has been patiently hovering. See you in Grotto 104." Dr. Oiseau transforms into her human form and says, "Yes, thank you Professor Gustaf. It is always inspiring to hear your explanations."

Dr. Oiseau takes a seat on a lounge chair, crosses her legs, and continues: "Some of our current healing methods take this concept of harmonics into account incorporating various energy ranges to invoke natural healing. Color therapy uses colored light to induce self-healing. Acupuncture uses fine stainless steel needles to bypass and clear energy blockages in the meridians while acupressure uses pressure at critical nodes on the meridian lines for similar results. Some practitioners place crystals on the energy centers. And, of course, you saw how Quantum K uses some of these energetically. The phenomena of healing energies can also be generated by <u>thought</u>. Thinking produces a thought form energy that resonates throughout the lattice which is directly connected to your DNA."

"Ester Hicks of Abraham-Hicks fame channels through the group entity known as Abraham who states that humans <u>are</u> creators. This seems to be in agreement with the Bible (Psalms 82.6) that says we are gods, does it not? As creators we constantly express our thoughts as wants and release these thoughts (or prayers) into the universal lattice. Abraham calls these thoughts 'rockets of desire.'"

"Mystics of long ago taught that thinking results in thought forms or bundles of energy, that given sufficient power can extend beyond one's immediate aura field. Thoughts without emotional energy or intent remain with the sender but thoughts filled with emotion cause a residual effect in the sender's energy field. Of course, if these are negative thoughts such as anger, they can have serious health consequences to the sender. The thoughts you harbor in your mind are ***critical*** to your well being."

"So here is how it works. You create a thought. This thought has an energy pattern or composite frequency which harmonically produces frequencies at multiple levels including those which might harmonize with your heart, brain, lungs and other body components. Both positive and negative thoughts will influence your physical well being. So before creating a thought-form, consider its effect on your physical body. If you have difficulty thinking 'positive' when things are not going your way, make an extra effort to find some positive aspect of the situation or if necessary invent something positive. Why? Thinking of something positive will not only alleviate your mind, it will actually <u>attract</u> positive energy and improve the overall outcome."

"A thought or desire is simply a form of energy. The thought resonates within the lattice, activated through your awareness of its existence or from intense prayer, and travels into points of light. Like a wave in an ocean, your thought is set in motion and travels in all directions throughout the universe; the universe automatically responds to the energy in accordance with the impartial principles of yin and yang and the Laws of the Universe. Professor Muhlaton will offer more details on this in Grotto 105."

"How do we actually know thoughts <u>do</u> anything? Fortunately, today's science can back that up with experimentation. Twenty-first century Japanese scientist Masaru Emoto's work with water demonstrated how positive and negative thoughts affect water crystallization. In several published experiments, a group of students would send thoughts of grace and love to one bowl of water and negative thoughts to another. After freezing, the resultant crystals from the two groups were clearly different, one with a distorted shape and the other with a beautifully balanced structure. See the examples below provided by the office of Mr. Emoto."

Water Crystal of Thank You, ©Office Masaru Emoto, LLC

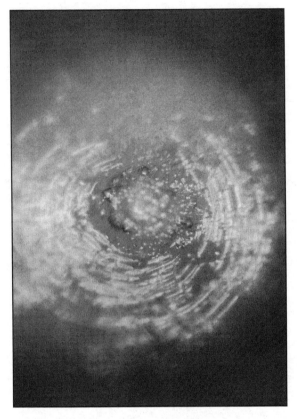

Water Crystal of You Fool, ©Office Masaru Emoto, LLC

So…
Life is all about

THOUGHT

'I think therefore I am'
&
'You are what you think'

are NOT frivolous statements.

They are at the heart of being human.

Great Thoughts on
THOUGHT

"Each of us has powers of which we are unaware ... Our limitations are the product of our own thinking and self-evaluation. If only we think, we can!"

By Ethel Percy Andrus, Founder, AARP

Xenophanes, a philosopher during the era of Pythagoras circa 500 B.C. said, *"The deity caused all things by the thought of his mind."*

Marcus Aurelius, emperor of Rome in 160 AD said, *"The happiness of your life depends on the quality of your thoughts."*

And from a poem entitled 'THINK' by the Qatar Foundation (www.qf.org.qa), published in TIME magazine of 5/17/2010:

> *"What makes a Thought so powerful*
> *Is that it can be created by anybody.*
> *At anytime.*
> *From anywhere."*

And now 2000 years later, we can say, "*We are co-creators of reality with God.*"

"With that thought, we will look at the workings of the universe and see how thought can create our world. Understand this and your magic will be potent."

THINK THOUGHT

Think Green, GO
Think Red, STOP
Think Power, DO

Think Thought, CREATE
Think big, Create BIG

Thought can move mountains,
Thought can heal wounds,
Thought can build trust,

Thought can express LOVE;

What is your thought?
Is it for GOOD?
Or is it for Naught?

Thought you can GIVE and thought you can KEEP,
But Thought always will MANIFEST!

Let it be POSITIVE, never Negative…

For what you THINK,

IS

©M. Eisenbacher

Grotto 104:
Magic of Science

Current science was yesterday's magic;
today's magic is tomorrow's science

Professor Gustaf von Lichtenstein, a tall lean man with a relaxing but demanding demeanor, marches onto the stage with exceptionally long silver hair expanding outward from his head like lightning bolts, his silvery beard pointing outward, and his full mustache a matching sliver of silver. He addresses us with a broad smile: "It is good to see you again." He pauses, and then adds "The world you came into is filled with magic. As we grow into adults, we are trained to see the world with blinders in order to obtain approval of adults in the world *they* understand. We now want to open your awareness quotient by reminding you of the magic already in this world, the current magic of science, recent creations by science, and the magic of future possibilities."

"Let's consider the natural world and its miracles. The most apparent is the miracle of birth. From a tiny seed, the embryonic system 'knows' from its DNA how to build itself into a full form. All forms of life from human to the weed are governed by their DNA, the blueprint containing the instructions for the growth of each unique cell within the organism of life. Ponder this for a moment. Consider how the parts of the human, from blood cells to nerves to organs to limbs are all coordinated second by second by your brain, heart, and glands. Is that not truly miraculous in itself? And let's not forget the unique ability of a human to stand and balance on two sticks (legs) three feet above the ground. A robot that can lift itself and stand like a human has not yet been created."

"Consider the myriad forms of beauty on our biological planet. Ever notice how cute miniature versions of all life forms are, including animals (like humans), birds, and even bugs ... or the amazing colors of flowers on this planet, or the multitudes of water creatures in existence? Visit an aviary or an aquarium and notice the myriad colors in the birds' feathers or in the fish scales. Watch the transformation of caterpillars into colorful graceful butterflies."

"Our planet gifts us with an array of seasons—new born fledging plants in the spring, ripe fruits in the summer, multi-colored trees in the fall and crystalline snowflakes in winter. Beautiful examples of nature surround us everywhere, in all countries, among all cultures."

"The important point is to be consciously aware of life. Awareness of life's positive vibrations tends to simultaneously stimulate positive vibrations in you. Enjoy the world you live in—there is none other like it."

"Thousands of years ago man arrived on the scene and has been 'creating' ever since. More recently in the last hundred years, man has made major leaps in scientific progress. Imagine, if you were to transport any of today's electronic devices into Merlyn's time at King Arthur's Court, it would have been considered serious magic and you might have been burned as a witch. Had you lived in the Middle Ages and someone showed you a 10 inch box with people and whole cities in it or a device you hold in your hand which has voices and music coming out of it, even entire musical groups (iPod®) or watch a written letter being pulled into a box and come out at another box a distance away (FAX) or see a flat paper displaying a map of your city with moving markers showing positions of people and places (iPad®/ Google Maps), you would have been both impressed and frightened with such magic. You would cause a public scene if you placed a potato in a metal box and without even lighting a fire, retrieve it fully cooked in a few minutes. How magical is that?"

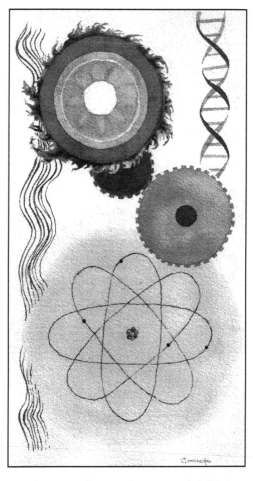

The Magic of Energy (A. Domineske) (TV)

"Cars, airplanes, and telephones did NOT exist 140 years ago. Our airplanes have become jets, telephones have evolved into cell phones, and cars are morphed into hybrid vehicles. Hospitals 100 years ago were places of care; today they are marvels of technology providing us with replacement knees, hips, transplanted kidneys and hearts, all with high tech robotic instruments and lasers."

"Today's technology is expanding at an ever faster rate— in the near future we may see miniature machines known as nanobots inside your body fixing failing organs a molecule at a time, devices providing instant communication across light years of space, medical facilities regenerating body limbs using techniques of fractal healing, and governments offering long distance travel through wormhole portals. Which of these will you take part in?"

We need more wizards.

"Since the DNA is a holographic blueprint of your body where each cell has the coded information for an entire body, regeneration of body parts is theoretically possible <u>now</u>."

We need more wizards.

"Anything imagined is potentially possible. It is a fact that the majority of innovations are created by young minds not yet locked in their thinking processes."

The world needs more wizards.

"The wizard knows things aren't always what they seem. Some things we all see but not see. Look at the photo below. Do you see the tree and water? Most do."

CAN YOU SEE?

"But do you see the baby? Look again, once you see it you can't not see it."

"How many things do we see in this world yet not see? <u>Awareness</u> of this fact opens our mind to see more."

Don't be so quick to judge what you do
not see or even what you do see!

"Even when you and I see the same things, each will perceive it differently due to our own unique history while living on this world. Below is a photo of a _____?"

What do You see?

"If you said frog, you are correct: if you said horse, you are correct. If you only see one of these, rotate the picture counterclockwise. You can't always be sure that what you see is the whole picture."

Consider other peoples' version of truth before dismissing them as false or wrong.

"Be aware of other possibilities."

"Our minds tend to be encased in fortresses of knowledge. We place information in 'boxes' to categorize them. This is inherent in the nature of linear thinking and linear teaching. This generation, i.e. *YOU*, however, are more adaptable to thinking beyond these boxes; rather, you tend to grasp the whole thought rather than learn in a step by step fashion. Actually you could learn Grotto 103 and 104 simultaneously if we were able to present information in that fashion."

We need more wizards.

"So now let's stretch our minds a little. Is this world real? What is reality? These questions are not new; they were posed by the great Greek philosophers like Aristotle, Plato, and Socrates. Are we living in a lucid dream? Will we wake up 100 years from now? Will we enter another lucid dream after we 'die'? Or are we a computer simulation in 3D, operated by creatures in 4D, manipulating our lives? Or are we living on an electron spinning around a nucleus? The possibilities are endless."

"What did the Wizards of our past have to say about reality? Heraclitus in 600 B.C. thought of reality as a process of ever changing flux, expanding and contracting, mirroring the oriental concept of yin and yang. Parmenides in 500 B.C. reasoned that the nature of reality must be an undivided single entity and therefore changes are an illusion. Renè Descartes in the 17th century said the only sure thing is 'I think therefore I am' and claimed our beliefs are derived from our senses and perception. He concluded there is no way to tell the difference between reality and dreaming. Einstein in the 20th century showed that the observer is important in the process of perception; he produced the first evidence that <u>humans can affect matter directly</u>."

"Let's see what science acknowledges of our strange world. At one time philosophers such as Democritus in 400 B.C. and John Dalton in early 19th century had conjectured the existence of atoms and electrons, now taught in Science 101. Ancient mystics taught principles of opposites while today science concedes that matter and antimatter, electrons and positrons, suns and dark holes actually exist."

"Are <u>we</u> thinking out of the box? It is time to include our hearts, our intuition, and the non-logic part of the brain in our thinking process. Look for possibilities not encased in mental fortresses.

The Wizards you saw in the magical mirror in Grotto 102 <u>do</u> think out of the box. Did you see yourself in that mirror?"

"Since Galileo's time in early 17ᵗʰ century, science has shown us that our planet which we now call Gaia is no longer the center of the world but is one planet in one solar system in one galaxy in one universe among many. We know as large the universe is to us, so too, we are to the smallest particles of our world. The range of physics disciplines has expanded from the smallest with nano-technology to the largest with the cosmology of the universe. In the Quantum world of subatomic particles science has discovered that particles are no longer particles but packets of energy that exist as matter only when observed, otherwise they are only probabilities. This means science has acknowledged that consciousness has a say in the existence of particles, or in other words, mind can create matter."

"Is this magic? Or is this the true nature of our world? Are we all magicians and just don't know how to use our powers? That is probably closer to the truth than we realize."

"Science of the past studied nature, observed consistent behavior and through experimentation determined the formulas or classical laws of physics. In today's scientific world of Quantum energy, the researcher studies the mathematics of the problem and from that determines the possibilities before experimenting to prove the derived formula. An example is Pythagoras theorem of the right triangle. If you put the triangle in 3D space and add another side, it can be rotated in space such that the sum of the areas of the sides always equals the area of the hypotenuse. Physicists ask the question mathematically how many edges or dimensions can be created and still maintain Pythagoras' Law. So far, from this mathematical experiment, theoretical physicists have concluded that at least eleven dimensions are possible."

"Now let's get back to our DNA and invite Dr Oiseau to share this class with us." Dr. Robyn Oiseau appears to us as a wise Owl with grey and red feathers, "Yes, please proceed with what I started in Grotto 103."

Professor Gustaf continues, "Remember, DNA contains the holographic code of man—including that of all of his bodies, physical, mental, spiritual and the god within. The physical DNA consists of a double helix connected with ladder rungs of chromosomes. Science has identified perhaps 5% of the total strand and calls the balance 'junk' DNA."

Dr. Oiseau interjects, "You and I know the creator does not create a complex structure like the DNA with the majority of it as junk; nature has a purpose for everything and is never wasteful. Kryon, through Lee Carroll, has stated that the junk DNA is the link or the instruction set for the other eleven layers (there's that *'twelve'* again). Now that's a Hoot!"

Gustaf continues, "Now consider what this may mean. Assume humans can operate in twelve dimensions simultaneously, and if the coding inherent in the DNA is connected at all times to eleven other dimensions, what does this say about the human potential? Yes, humans can connect through the DNA with each other across time, space and even dimensions."

"Viewing the human body through the eyes of your multi-dimensional self (See the next graphic) reveals the seven energy vortices of the chakra system plus two vortices, one above and one below the physical form, *twelve* circular strands connecting the ends forming an egg shape, AND several figure-eight strands of energy connecting these nine vortices to the twelve strands circling the human figure. Each strand might be associated with a particular dimension. Aren't humans truly amazing?!"

UNIVERSAL CALIBRATION LATTICE® by Peggy Phoenix Dubro

[Authors note: This graphic, conceptually similar to the Rave chart from Grotto 102, displays the Universal Calibration Lattice® as described by Peggy Phoenix Dubro—please see the Crypt for further information.]

"Getting back to Physics. Scientists since Einstein have been searching for a unified theory of the universe. The Universal Calibration Lattice® may be the answer. The lattice is not a grid nor is it God. It is, however, God's tool that connects everything together. It is God's power of love and OUR source of power, literally. Within this lattice, power is timeless and spaceless; it is both positive and negative, consisting of both yin and yang energies; it is a Null state in perfect balance where matter and anti-matter can exist simultaneously; it is the Buddhist VOID from which all things are created by consciousness. It is the Vortex from which we spring forth and return."

"The current studies of Quantum consider string theory as the new unified field where strings of force are like spaghetti strands-- flexible, vibrating, yet directional. Science may yet discover the lattice and harness its unlimited power for the benefit of mankind."

We need more wizards.

Our favorite owl, heron, and hummingbird appears once more in human form and summarizes with, "Humans are unique in that we are connected directly to the lattice and can control our DNA with Intent and Love. Anything is possible for the human of the 21st century."

With that Professor Gustaf and Dr Oiseau disappear in a puff of smoke.

Grotto 105:
Secrets of Magic

Setting: Studio with a couch, two lounge chairs,
two bookends and two podiums

The entrance to Grotto 105 is a long tunnel deep into the earth's consciousness. Upon arriving, we find ourselves in a radio recording studio. Surrounding the two podiums in the center are two 6 foot bookends with human heads dangling over the top. Suddenly lights flash above and circles of light appear over the left bookend. To everyone's amazement its head wakes up and it says, "Good morning Chet". The light moves to the other bookend. Its head bobs up and responds, "Good morning Dave".

Dave then announces, "Students of Wizardry, may I present the honorable Headmaster Muhlaton. With the sound of trumpets, the Headmaster descends from the ceiling above gliding slowly to the center podium. The Headmaster is dressed in a flowing robe of violet, a golden scepter in his left hand and a ring on each of three fingers of his right hand, "I have asked Chet and Dave of historical fame to monitor a Question and Answer session."

DAVE: Professor Muhlaton, please summarize how these novices have been prepared for the magical process you will present today.

HM: (Headmaster Muhlaton): Upon entrance to this school they have been shown the significance of history and numbers in the magical world. They understand the value of learning both new and old concepts. They have indicated that they have a love and respect for education and agree to maintain an open mind to new ways of thinking.

DAVE: And?

HM: These novices have been presented with the way of the witch and wizard. They have been encouraged to respect all cultures while acknowledging their differences. They are ready to enter the Wizard community.

HM: Furthermore, they have been introduced to the concepts of energy fields and have an understanding of how thought energy can affect all aspects of life anywhere, everywhere, and anytime. They have been introduced to the concepts of science and have ideas of the potential of future science.

DAVE: Then you do declare the novices are ready to learn the procedures of magic?

HM: These students are ready.

DAVE: Professor Muhlaton, we would like to begin this session with questions received from your students. May we begin?

HM: By all means. As you direct your questions, I will have the appropriate instructor appear instantly at the instructor podium.

DAVE: Professor. Are Wizards more valued than most humans?

HM: No, we all have a place in the mechanism of the Universe. We are all part of the tapestry of the lattice. Wizards are light workers with unique responsibilities; they carry the torch for mankind. All others are place holders each with a special mission. All humans are angels incarnate and are part of the human tapestry. One out of place broken strand disrupts a whole tapestry; so too, each individual/angel is critical to the functioning of the whole. We are all joined together in the lattice to carry humanity forward, for it is the humans on this planet, as spirit beings, who will affect the <u>entire</u> universe of beings in all worlds, dimensions, past, present, and future.

DAVE: Professor Muhlaton: What do you fear the most?

HM: I am concerned about the economic upheaval when mankind no longer needs pharmaceuticals or the medical establishment as we know it today. I am also concerned about the effects on social security financials when the government realizes future man can live several hundred years. Then there's the shock to the oil industry when scientists discover how to tap into the VOID for an infinite supply of power.

DAVE: Dr. Oiseau, What is the new science of *epigenetics*?

DO (Dr. Oiseau): This is the study of changes in gene expression caused by external signals or attachments to the DNA called methylation that modifies the functions of the DNA without actually altering the DNA. The instructions sent to the DNA define which genes are to be active, possibly for one or more generations. For example, it might send the signal that predisposes Alzheimer's. This science can lead to physical manipulation of the signals to the DNA as a precursor to using our thoughts to transmit instructions to the DNA directly through the universal lattice.

DAVE: Professor Muhlaton, since magic is attributed to thought, are we creating our own reality through thought?

HM: Yes. At some level, we are creating our physical world, albeit much of it is by consensus reality, i.e., we all agree on specific aspects of the physical. On the individual level, we do create the reality of our lives and everyday events. In essence we are totally responsible for our life; we cannot blame others or providence; it is our own thinking that gets us where we are.

DAVE: Professor Gustaf. Is dimensional travel possible?

PG (Professor Gustaf): There is some report that a Russian microbiologist has proved that the DNA can create abnormal electronic wormholes in a vacuum—this may be the precursor to portal travel (as in the science fiction movie *Stargate*). Watch the news.

DAVE: Sister Sulis. What is the value of meditation?

SS (Sister Sulis): It calms the outer mind and opens the communication channels through the universal lattice.

DAVE: Sister Sulis. How does the 100th monkey theory fit into our studies?

SS: 1987 was the beginning of the earths' magnetic shift and the Harmonic Convergence; since then the communication link through the lattice to our DNA has begun to open. This will open fully when the critical mass reaches Wizard status, which according to Sheldrake's Morphic Resonance Theory, is one tenth of 1% of the world's population (1 of every 1000 persons) or seven million people, about the size of New York City. This is why we need more Wizards and why I asked the authors to create this manual and synchronized website.

DAVE: Dr. Oiseau. How is the soul history in each person's DNA affected by mating?

HM: I will answer this one. We know that the first level of the DNA is integrated as new DNA at childbirth. As for the multi-dimension levels including the records of past lives, we as yet do not know the actual mechanism. A good reason for more Wizards.

DAVE: Dr. Oiseau. If the DNA of a baby can create new limbs in the womb, why can't we replace damaged or missing limbs?

DO: Until now the communication link between our minds and our DNA has been sealed. Since 1987 this connection has been gradually opening, improving the efficiency of the DNA's healing system. In time, this will be the norm.

DAVE: The following questions are directed at you, Headmaster. What is the most important component of Magic?

HM: Intent, intent, and intent. It is by far the most important component. As Descartes had said, "I think therefore I am" is all we can be sure about; it is the key to being human. It is the basis of all existence. Without thought nothing can exist. In fact, for everything in existence there was first a thought, *then* the creation. Anything you make, build, or bake must first be imagined and thought through, does it not? So it is with Magic.

HM: It is agreed that we all have fleeting thoughts which do not result in any particular creation because there is no intent behind it. It is the thoughts that we dwell on and inadvertently or intentionally give intent to, that manifest in an event. So if you think and say something negative about your life consistently and believe it, you are giving that thought intent; you are essentially creating a spell against yourself. A thought with intent alerts the universe which will *automatically comply with your wishes however stated*; the universe places no judgment. Is that clear? Positive or negative thoughts will result in a similar consequential event.

DAVE: What is the power behind magic?

HM: Emotions. This is the <u>second</u> most important component of magic. The stronger the emotion behind the intent, the higher the probability of the thought becoming manifested. The strongest emotion that aligns with the lattice is Love, the kind of love that includes compassion and the universal feeling and knowing of being part of the Universal system. The more emotion of this kind you can feel, the more powerful the intent.

DAVE: We don't always feel 'positive' emotions. Sometimes we are just downright angry. How can we manifest Magic if we can't get into the love emotion?

HM: That is a great question, Dave. Granted it is not easy under those conditions. Did you know that humans are born with an *emotional guidance system*? Your feelings are always along a spectrum of emotions from very angry to depressed to discontented to apathetic to interested to content to happy to ecstatic. Get the picture? So, the best way to improve your feelings is to move them up the emotional scale. Even a slight move in the right direction makes you feel a little better which then has the effect of attracting more positive feelings (and events); for example, you may feel anger first but with a little effort you can improve it to depressed and so on until you can release a positive thought. Each movement in the upward direction will attract more positive feelings.

So if you cannot think clearly enough to think something positive about your situation, imagine something way-out possible, as if you were creating a fairy tale. 'It is the thought that counts'. Remember that cliché? Remember too that 'Fairy Tales do come true'. The results may not come out exactly the way you imagine but it starts the ball rolling in your favor. Then synchronicity takes over.

DAVE: So what makes magic happen is synchronicity?

HM: Yes. Synchronicity means that the universe responds to your request, prayer, or intent in a synchronistic fashion rather than directly. Your thought may wish a certain outcome, for example more money. The thought form enters the Universal lattice surrounding your DNA and instantly transmits through the lattice everywhere effecting things, events, and people. The combined energy resonates with energies conducive to your request and shows up in many ways—as opportunities you can pursue, ideas you might apply, people you need to see, places you should go, events which create other events or simply avenues never before considered. Of course, you must be alert to the possibilities that show up and then respond appropriately. Expecting money to fall from the sky is simply not the way it works. On the flip side of this, if the intent is not clear or based on the *lack* of something, the Universe will still respond to what you are thinking; being impartial, the universe will respond with more '*lack*' assuming that is what you want since you are putting so much emphasis on that. So be mindful of your intent and how you express it internally.

DAVE: The last question is for Sister Sulis. Why were there so few Wizards in the magic mirror of Grotto 102?

SS: Those were the ones that the class could currently <u>see</u>. There are many more in there.

DAVE: Thank you, Professor Muhlaton. At this point, we suggest an intermission, after which we would like you to review the magical process step by step. Meanwhile Chet would like to interview the authors who have invited us to this session.

HM: Thank you, I am looking forward to it.

CHET: Thank you Dave.

* * *

Setting: As the Headmaster leaves the podium to retire to the background, we find seated on the two lounge chairs Mr. Mario Garnet and Ms. Tamara Starr.

CHET: Mr. Garnet, I understand you have had experiences with magic at an early age. Would you care to share one of your experiences with us?

MG (Mario Garnet): Chet, please call me Mario. Yes, I would love to share an early experience with magic. Of course at the time I did not realize it but looking back it was a prime example. I was sixteen and just joined a mystical order with my mother's permission. So, I guess in some ways my thoughts were linked with the cosmic lattice or cosmic consciousness as it was called then.

I was a normal high school teenager wanting freedom that a vehicle could give me. Since a car was out of the question, and I was still underage in my state, I started dreaming of motor scooters. While my father was stationed in Germany, I had seen many teenagers driving around in motorized bikes commonly called mopeds.

So I went to the library and discovered the Vespa, an Italian motor scooter that actually operated without a bike chain as so many did. The design intrigued me. I found several manuals in the library written in British English. I read the books over and over until I could almost feel the Vespa under me. I had no idea how I could obtain one. I never saw one in the USA and surely never saw one in any motorcycle store.

My intent was clear. My passion was strong. I really, really wanted a Vespa. Then like Magic, it suddenly appeared in our new Sears Roebuck Catalog. Now you must understand my parents shopped a lot at Sears; we received the catalogs regularly and I always probed the Sears Christmas 'Wishbook' to create my holiday wish list. So the rest is history. What was magical was that Sears never sold a Vespa or any Piaggio product until that spring, exactly when I really wanted one. Of course after that year, it was never sold by Sears again.

Is that a coincidence or what? As you discover with Magic, there are no coincidences, only synchronistic events. I am still fond of the Vespa to this day.

CHET: well that's quite a story. Thank you for sharing your experience.

MG: It definitely showed me the possibility of intent and belief. Even at an early age, I realized anything is possible.

CHET: Ms. Starr, as an illustrator for children's books, what inspired you to take on this work?

TS (Tamara Starr): When Mario shared his synopsis with me I was immediately inspired, not only by the message but by his passion and excitement. It was clear that we met for a reason. I normally paint for young children and was excited at the opportunity to darken things up and show another side to my art.

CHET: Ms. Starr, Your art is sometimes dark but always expressive. Why is that?

TS: I tried to match the tone of the Harry Potter adventure. Notice that Mario starts the book with light storytelling and adds increasingly more information as he goes deeper into the topics. Ms Rowling's work also started as the story of a boy and evolved into darker subjects as he grew into a young adult. I am keeping in line with that philosophy.

CHET: Tamara. Have you had any 'out of the box' experiences?

TS: Yes, Many. One of the most memorable happened while I was meditating. It was as if I was transported through time and space to the center of God's heart. It was a place of pure love where I was connected to everything and everyone and life had no questions, no answers, it just was. I could see how perfect we all are; I felt my energy was entwined with God, with the universe, with everything that is. I was pure energy and pure love. This is heaven I thought, it must be. When you have experienced something like this, when you have touched God and have felt love in its full strength... nothing ever seems the same. We are all perfect, beautiful, talented and full of magic.

CHET: Thank you Tamara. Mario, you live on the East Coast and Ms Starr, you live on the West Coast. Could you share how you two connected?

MG: That is truly a case of the Magic of synchronicity. My desire to complete this work was active in the lattice and while conducting business with a company she worked for, I brought up the concept of this book and discovered she was not only emotionally in alignment with my goals, she was a published illustrator and could tune to my energy. I knew she could reflect in pictures what I was feeling. Furthermore, I did a quick numerology check of our pen names and discovered they both equal a '4', the number for stability and completeness. That clinched it for me.

CHET: Thank you, Mario and Tamara for presenting your work to the world. Of course, there may be critics who object to revealing this knowledge. Are you prepared for that?

MG: I am looking forward to critics. They generate more interest and add to the validity of this work. Regardless of individual belief systems, the intent of this work is to create Wizards who can change the world for the better. What better time than now—the earth has made a magnetic shift and the Mayan calendar says 2012 is the year of the new beginning.

TS&MG: We hope that we are making a positive impact on our world.

CHET: Thank you. Back to you Dave.

DAVE: [nodding at the Professor]. Please continue with your presentation.

Mario and Tamara leave the stage as the Headmaster Professor Muhlaton rises to the podium, takes a sip of water and begins.

HM: I am very pleased to do so for this most honorable and worthy class. To Mario and Tamara, I appreciate your intent in introducing this School of Wizardry to the Universe.

HM: Dave, These are simple rules; do not underestimate their power.

First. Define your ***Intent***. Ask yourself why you are creating this thought. What result are you expecting? Do not think about *how* it will happen, just focus on the end *result*. Allow the universe to work for you. The system will gather the resources and lay out the events for you.

Second. **Visualize** the results with clarity. Do this using as many senses as possible. *See* the details in your mind; it helps to create them as if it were a 3D dream. *Feel* the sensations you expect to feel when you attain the results. Imagine the result is in current time, like it already exists. If appropriate, add smells and sounds to your image. Immerse yourself in the desire or thought for at least seventeen (17) seconds. Think from your heart (intuitive sensing) instead of your brain (linear thinking). Scientific studies have shown that the electromagnetic (EMF) energy from the heart is hundred times more powerful that from the brain.

Third: **Release** the thought to the Universe with **emotion**—love and gratitude; *trust* that the energy will direct itself to all the right places. This means letting go of the thought. Stop the intense focus. You may meditate or simply get on with the affairs of your life.

Fourth: Let **synchronicity** do its work through the Law of Attraction. During your day, unusual thoughts, events, or opportunities will appear unexpectedly. Take note and follow your instincts. Take advantage of what the universe places before you—it is no accident. There are no coincidences, only synchronistic events.

Fifth: Practice, practice, and practice. During our next session we will introduce exercises to hone your ability.

DAVE: Thank you Professor, we are looking forward to it.

HM: Thank you and Good Night. We will meet in the Grand Hall for the graduation ceremonies.

As the studio clears, the lights dim ... we hear:

DAVE: Good Night, Chet

CHET: Good Night, Dave

ILLUMINATO:
The Practice of Magic

Even wizards have a sense of Humor. (T. Starr)

Swarms of students are entering the great expanse of the ceremonial hall. Each group of twelve is seated on a wedge shaped platform, one of twelve, stacked twelve high, all facing a center stage in the round. The entire assembly is inside a giant crystalline sphere with holographic properties where the stage appears directly in front of each person.

Suddenly all lights are out with only the stage visible in light from some unknown source. In a poof of smoky light, Headmaster Muhlaton appears in his best regalia—a full gown of crimson velvet trimmed with gold highlighted by his natural radiant glow. Atop his head is the formal wizard's hat of the same velvet texture, its point rounded just right. Positioned over his heart is the high spiritual symbol of the *Merkaba*—two geometric pyramids interlaced with one point up and other pointing down resulting in an eight point star.

As he raises his hands over his head with palms forward, you can hear the hush of silence. "Welcome to this great event. You are the first graduating class of this wizardry school having completed the first phase of becoming a wizard. At this stage we would like to honor your instructors and the knowledge they imparted."

"Mr. Henderson," the Headmaster calls out, nodding to his right, Mr. Henderson emerges into our dimension from a rip in the time space continuum, wearing his fanciest Renaissance outfit, light green blouse with frills at the wrists, dark green pantaloons to just below his knees tied around green stockings, black pumps, and a green woolen jacket with large lapels, the left one displaying the Wizard's symbol ∞.

"Sister Sulis," announces the Headmaster. Sulis floats through the dimensional rip, arriving in her best formal witch's attire, a full length iridescent black cloak, pointed black hat with a wide brim, black granny type boots, and a wand in hand with a pentagram at the tip. On her cloak over her right breast are two adjacent half moons, one waxing and one waning, the moon edges pointing to the sides.

"Dr Robyn Oiseau," as she glides through the same opening, appearing in a gown of pastel blue feathers that lift her slightly off the floor, her head adorned with a blue hat of peacock feathers giving the impression of eyes on her head. On her chest is the familiar ancient medieval symbol of the medical profession, the caduceus, a two-headed snake wrapped around a staff plus a dodecahedron representing the twelve layers of DNA.

As Professor Gustaf von Lichtenstein is announced, a distinguished looking gentleman with a diminutive beard in a dark grey form-fitting business suit appears. On his jacket lapel is the insignia of a six pointed star created from two superimposed equilateral triangles pointing to the heavens and to the earth.

While looking at the students, the Headmaster waves his right hand pointing towards the instructors, "Our distinguished staff ..." To the instructors' surprise, the students rise in their seats, clapping with such gusto that it brought tears of pride to their eyes.

As the fervor dies down and everyone is seated, "We are all here together today to honor our novice wizards as they complete the circle of their training and transcend into a new beginning."

"During your journey, Mr. Henderson imparted to you the importance of your history and the magical value of numbers in our universe. Sister Sulis showed you a vision of the Wizard's culture of diversity. Dr. Oiseau impressed you with the interconnectedness of life, the complexity of the DNA, and the power of thought while Professor Gustaf demonstrated the validity of a vibrational universe and the promise of science and magic intertwining into possibilities heretofore unimagined. And I provided the step by step procedure for projecting your thoughts effectively. Together, we believe you are ready for the next stage of ritual Magic in preparation for the graduation ceremony."

With a wave of his hand, the center stage clears into an open space. "In this stage, we will create a sacred space and perform some basic rituals and experiments designed to enhance your connection with spirit and improve your propensity for Magic."

Creating a Sacred Space

Sister Sulis takes the podium and explains, "A ritual is your personal connection to the Universal Lattice known by others as the Divine Consciousness or Supreme Creator. To create your sacred space, you may wish to design a makeshift altar consisting of a table or shelf with statues of a god, goddess, animal, favorite historical character or whatever trinkets such as crystals or stones help you 'feel' the sacredness of your environment. You may also wish to add a form of symbolic light such as an electronic candle (safe), night light, or some other low light. You may wish to use incense or a perfume spray that has a lingering smell to give your sacred space a sensory memory."

"In many cases a physical altar may not be possible or desirable. An excellent option is to create a Virtual Ritual Space in your mind. Visualize a defined space with all the objects you wish in it. Each time you need to be in the sacred space, repeat the same vision. After a while, a dozen times or so, you will only need to say to yourself, 'I am in my ritual space' and your mind will automatically create the space and atmosphere. At first, rituals may seem to take time, but actually they need only take a split second; remember, time is a variable reality; once a ritual is created in your mind, you are there. The sacred space, physical or virtual, will enhance your ritual, be it a directed thought or one of the exercises to follow, or simply a moment of peaceful interlude with the Universe."

Energy Flow

Professor Gustaf takes the podium; lights darken around us—only his hands are visible, "As described in your studies, Chi energy flows continuously through your body's meridians. In this experiment you will see evidence of the energy within you."

Sit quietly, feet apart resting on the floor, hands held cupped in front of you relaxed, fingers touching, thumb to thumb, index finger to index finger, so as to create a space between your palms. Pull your hands apart such that there is about an inch of space between your fingers. Take 3 deep breaths and exhale deeply to relax. Now take a deep breath and hold it comfortably while you look at your hands in a soft focus at the center between the palms. To achieve a soft focus look at the whole space at once, not at a particular point. This gets easier after a little practice. Notice the spaces between the fingertips. You will see a field around each finger tip and sparks like lightning energy jump across them. You may bring your fingers closer down to ¼" at first, and then separate them out as long as you can see sparks.

Intuition

Dr. Oiseau takes the stand, "We would like you to improve your connection with the Universe by developing your intuitive capabilities. One of the common practices is to be alert to your inner response when your phone rings. This is not guessing based on logic, but a knowing by your inner consciousness and feeling.

It is often the first thought in your mind before it has time to rationalize who it might be based on hopes, past experience, or logic. The more you practice the more you will be correct, the greater your confidence, the more developed your intuition. It becomes a reliable 6th sense."

Directing Thought

"One of my favorite ways of directing thought is to mentally send your self a wake-up call. If you have your alarm set to 7 am for example, set your 'mind' alarm to 6:55 am. You will wake up just before the alarm does. Practicing this also helps you tune into the lattice. Try it every night, it can't hurt. Be reasonable, however, do not get totally exhausted and try to wake up extra early. It may work, but in such cases the body may overrule you to satisfy its need for sleep. When sending yourself a message, use your senses of perception; seeing the clock hands in your mind at a specific time, saying to yourself 'I will awake feeling alert, refreshed, and ready to go.' Imagine yourself waking wide awake. It works."

Tuning Exercise

Professor Muhlaton now at the podium continues with the tuning exercise, "This exercise is designed to relax your body fully while providing it with positive healing allowing your consciousness to make a quality connection with the Universal lattice. This is best in a subdued and quiet environment while in a reclining pose. You may wish to repeat this often as you rest your head on your pillows for a good night's rest. It is acceptable to record these steps (using a tape, CD, or digital recorder) and play them back to your self. Let us proceed."

Suddenly all the chairs become recliners, lights dim and the only sound heard is the Headmaster's voice as he speaks slowly and pauses between each sentence. "Let's imagine the atmosphere around us consists of BLUE air. This blue light energy permeates your body as you relax with eyes closed. Focus on each part of your body as you follow my voice and its instructions. You may wish to read this first; then repeat it from memory. This process will get you very relaxed, so do not do this when driving or biking. Focus on the top of your head to the point of being fully aware and actually feeling it. Now let it relax on an exhale. Let the thought of it go. Focus on your face. Feel the facial muscles; be aware of your nose and ears. Sense the hair on your face and head. The more you can feel it, the more relaxed you get when letting go."

"Now focus on your neck likewise and let it go. Focus on your shoulders. Let them go. Relax your upper arms. Let them go. Relax you lower arms, your wrist, and your hands in a similar way. As you relax let the parts go loose and limp."

Now focus on your chest. Let it relax. Feel your buttocks; squeeze your muscles then let them go limp, relaxing even more.

"Tense your thigh muscles. Relax them. Tense your calves and relax them. Your whole body feels relaxed and possibly even a bit numb. Relax your ankles, then your heels, feet, and toes. Focus on each toe, and then release it. You are now perfectly relaxed."

"Now imagine a GREEN healing light energy floating over your body. Imagine the light flowing into the top of your head, over your face, and across your shoulders. As this light fills your body, each part becomes even more relaxed than before. Let it flow down your arms and into your hands, across your chest, waist and into your hips, as you relax even more. Finally let it flow into your legs and down to your feet and out your toes, carrying with it all your worries, fears, and stresses, letting you relax even more."

"Now imagine a GOLDEN bubble over your body. Watch it expand and absorb your being. As you relax, inhale the golden spiritual essence of the lattice. Feel it filling your body from the inside out, flowing through your legs and feet, filling your chest cavity, filling your head, supplying magical energy to every cell of your being. You feel peaceful and powerful and at one with the Universe."

Headmaster Muhlaton pauses a few minutes, and says, "As I count from 1 to 5 you will awaken, feeling alert and full of energy. 1... 2... 3... 4 5." Pausing in silence for a few moments, he then says, "Repeat this process as often as you wish to experience a deep relaxation. If you do this before bedtime, you may well fall asleep before you finish." The lights slowly brighten to full intensity as everyone awakens to present time.

After a few moments, Dr. Oiseau speaks, "We will now perform several mantras of immense value to your subconscious. A mantra is an affirmation repeated until it becomes the wisdom of the mind. Say these several times upon rising for your day until they are second nature."

"Please repeat these mantras with me ...
I am grateful. I am healthy and complete.
I am in harmony.
I harmonize with ... the unconditional love of the Universe.
I harmonize with ... the perfection and purity in all people.
I harmonize with ... abundance and happiness.
I harmonize with ... living in the moment
in accordance with my highest plan.

I am unique, beautiful, talented and lovable.

I accept that everything I do, feel and say on my life's path is part of my growth to higher states of understanding and consciousness."

"Please repeat these several times before proceeding."

Master Muhlaton pauses, then slowly rises to the podium and announces, "Ladies and Gentlemen, we will now begin the Graduation Ceremony."

The Commencement (T. Starr)

Commencement

Drums and trumpets blow announcing the moment. With a wave of the Headmaster's hand, the entire stage vanishes and a new stage appears within a large golden sphere. On the stage in five comfortable chairs, from left to right, are seated Mr. Henderson, Sister Sulis, Headmaster Muhlaton, Doctor Robyn Oiseau, and Professor Gustaf von Lichtenstein all in their finest attire.

The Headmaster rises and begins to say, "It is both with sadness and joy I stand before you today; sadness because we are at an end; joy because it is a new beginning. We have completed the journey of the circle ready to continue the spiral upward. You have completed the cycles of knowledge only to learn that learning is an ever expanding process; you have visited the cultures of man and acknowledged the divine nature of all men and women throughout time and space; you have seen inside the human body and realized the power within; you have visited the Universe and know the interconnectedness of time and space; you have learned the tools of magic and are now ready to accept the responsibility of this knowledge."

"Throughout the history of man, we have encountered heroes—Zeus in Ancient Greece, Jesus during the Dark Ages, Roy Rogers and Superman in the 50s, Luke Skywalker in the 70's and Harry Potter in the 21st century—all share in common the possibilities of who we can be. Today Stan Lee of Superheroes comic fame shows us on Discovery Channel actual modern humans with unique super powers, some gifted, some created; the possibilities of humans are endless."

"To you have been revealed some of the 'magic' techniques that are known only by the few, handed down from secret societies, indigenous cultures, and the pagan communities. With magic you will delve into the unknown and discover the things man only dreams about today. The only limits you encounter are those you create. The future rests with you, Wizards of the 21st century."

"You all wish to be successful. Success for you is not about money or prosperity, but doing something that inspires you to be the best you can be. Magic is the tool to help you achieve that. The value you will bring to the workplace is the value of learning; as your capacity increases, so too will your magical contributions and power."

"The future is full of promise. I see a world with universal clean energy sourced from the lattice, unlimited space exploration, instantaneous messaging, a balanced humanity, an international culture; all are possible in your lifetime. What part will you play? Remember, we only need one Wizard in each community of a thousand to effectively change the world."

Suddenly a bird flies into the Golden Bubble. The Headmaster says, "It is time". With that, the instructors rise from their seats and levitate upward forming the four corner base of a large pyramid with the Headmaster at its peak. As the bubble expands around the pyramid and slowly vibrates, the noble Phoenix zooms towards a large circular nest appearing in the center of the pyramid and with a sudden brake an inch above it, lands gracefully, absorbing residual negative energy from the students, as Headmaster Muhlaton booms, "We have been honored by the presence of the Phoenix and what she is about to do."

The golden bubble immediately expands to include all the students. Then to everyone's amazement the Phoenix's body explodes into spontaneous combustion.

"As the Phoenix returns to ashes, so too, goes the fate of your doubts, fears, weaknesses, poor thinking habits, and insecurities as they vaporize into oblivion."

The golden light vibrates to a very high rate and vanishes with a noisy snap; then it reappears as a soft glow emanating from each student individually, yet merging together as one.

Headmaster Muhlaton then asks, "For our closing ritual, please clasp your hands with fingers intertwined and say with us slowly the

Declaration of the Five Grottos"

As we declare each promise followed with an introspective pause, we watch the slow resurrection of the Phoenix as she rises from the ashes.

I promise to respect learning and continuously expand my consciousness.

I promise to respect persons of all belief systems and cultures.

I choose to consume vibrant food and drink, respect my body, and maintain my energy balance.

I promise to maintain awareness of the universal lattice and to always be prepared to think 'out of the box'.

I promise to Partner with my higher self in all future endeavors.

"As the Phoenix is reunited with the Lattice and complete, so too are you. So Mote it Be!""

"May I now present to the world...
The first official GRADUATES

Of

Muhlaton's School of Wizardry!

Go forth and prosper...

...Be More Than You Can Be.

Authenticator

The following questionnaire is located at www.muhlatonschoolof wizardry.com through the Authenticator portal. [The password through the portal is 'muhlaton'.] Complete the answers on the website correctly to receive your *Credentials of Mastery* Certificate attesting that you have read the <u>Wizard's</u> <u>Handbook</u> and completed the Grottos.

After the answers are automatically verified on the website as correct and you have been processed through PayPal with a small payment, the name you specified will be printed on the certificate in a high density PDF format (printable on photo quality paper) and emailed to the email address you provide. Optionally a printed copy is available. Your certificate includes your unique serial number which, after a short time period, will allow access through the *Wizard's Portal via the Eye* to apply for membership in the **Order of Wizardry.** This in turn will lead to further surprises!

Grotto: 101

Question #1: In this segment of the Fibonacci Series: 34, 55, 89, ___, what is the missing number?

A. 136
B. 144
C. 111
D. 55

Question #2: What is the ratio of two sides in a <u>Golden</u> Rectangle?

A. 3 to 1
B. 4 to 5
C. 1.16
D. Phi

Question #3: Who first said knowledge will set you free?

A. Henderson
B. Sulis
C. Socrates
D. Renoir

Grotto: 102

Question #4: There are only three active religions in this world, Judaism, Christianity, and Muslim. True or False?

A. True
B. False

Question #5: According to DNA studies where did all humans originally come from?

A. Africa
B. Fertile Crescent
C. Saudia Arabia
D. India
E. China

Question #6: Who was the originator of the 100th Monkey Theory?

A. Einstein
B. Sheldrake
C. Pythagoras
D. Euclid

Grotto: 103 & 104

Question #7: Of the 7 chakras in the Indian energy centers which of these is <u>not</u> one?

A. Crown
B. Stomach
C. Solar Plexus
D. Heart

Question #8: The Wizard does not need to be concerned with exercise, food, or sleep.

A. True
B. False

Question #9: Which of these birds does Dr. Oiseau <u>not</u> take form?

A. Heron
B. Robin
C. Owl
D. Hummingbird

Question #10: In the perception test, If it is not a frog, what is it?

A. Bug
B. Baby
C. Bird
D. Horse

Grotto: 105-

Question #11: What is the <u>second</u> most important element of magic?

A. Lies
B. Emotion
C. Affirmation
D. Decision

Question #12: Which of these teachers do not appear in the graduation ceremony?

A. Henderson
B. Oiseau
C. Plato
D. Gustaf

The Crypt

Preface:

The Harry Potter books by J. K. Rowling are at the top of this list—it is our source of inspiration for this book. Enjoy the entire set of books as well as the movies. Visit the virtual world of Hogsmeade at: www.universalorlando.com/harrypotter

You may also wish to visit the constructed site at Disney World!

Visit our website for the links referenced: www.muhlatonschoolofwizardry.com

Including our Facebook page at www.facebook.com/wizardshandbook

Grotto 101:

The Teaching Company is an excellent source for college level courses on numerous subjects including history and mathematics. Courses are provided in audio CD or tape format and DVD video format. Information is available at www.teach12.com

In particular we cite *Joy of Mathematics* as presented by Professor Arthur T.Benjamin of Harvey Mudd College for his amazing enthusiasm for mathematics and his flair for magical numbers.

For a Source of an in-depth study of Fibonacci numbers see Mario Livio's Book, _The Golden Ratio._

For live courses, consider attending a school of alternate studies with a collegiate-like campus such as Omega Institute in the Catskills of New York State. On-line information is available at www.eOmega.org

And yet another great source, Jean Houston's _Mystery School_, a school of human development, a program of cross-cultural, mythic and spiritual studies, dedicated to teaching history, philosophy, the New Physics, psychology, anthropology, myth and the many dimensions of human potential is presented at one of two retreat centers—New York or California. Detail information is available at www.jeanhouston.org

Grotto 102:

A wonderful source of religions including philosophies of the New Age is _The Joy of Sects_, a spirited guide to the World's religious traditions by Peter Occhiogrosso.

The source for the Astrology chart is the program _**Win Star**_ available through Matrix Software, Inc. at www.astrologysoftware.com

The story behind the Human Design System is best found at its UK origins, www.jovianarchive.com. The best place to find a listing of certified professionals in Human Design is at www. ihdschool.com/professionals.

Grotto 103:

The cited website for _**Quantum K**_ by kinesiologist and author Andrew J Kemp is: www.quantumk.co.uk

This site includes a fully documented FREE reference and a 23 minute healing session. The healing process is well worth experiencing.

The cited quote from Kryon is representative of the resources available through their web site at www.kryon.com

There are many Tai Chi groups in the US. Check out www.silvertigertaichi.com for Chinese Master Ting's unique approach to Tai Chi and Chi Gong emphasizing the principles of Yin and Yang, circular motion and the *feelings* of movement. Besides local classes, he offers monthly afternoon classes, and weekend seminar retreats as well as recorded lessons on DVD.

There are numerous resources for the study of the I-Ching and the Indian Chakra Systems. You may wish to use your search engine for these.

For real 'out of the box' exposure, consider the works of Abraham, published by Esther and Jerry Hicks. Esther channels truths from an alternate reality group called Abraham: Go to www.abraham-hicks.com for a wealth of information.

Masaru Emoto' s works are well presented in his book <u>Hidden Messages in Water</u>, translated by David A. Thayne, Beyond Words Publishing, 2004. His website is www.masaru-emoto.net

Grotto 104:

Rupert Sheldrake, one of the world's most innovative biologists and writers is best known for his theory of morphic fields and resonance described in his book <u>Morphic Resonance</u> available at www.amazon.com

Always fantastic are Gregg Braden's books including <u>The Divine Matrix</u>, <u>Spontaneous Healing of Belief</u>, and <u>Fractal Time</u> all available at Hay House publishing or at Amazon.com

Also consider the Teaching Company's course *Superstring Theory: The DNA of Reality* by Professor S. James Gates, Jr., University of Maryland.

An excellent reference book is Lynne McTaggart's book <u>The Field</u>: <u>The quest for the Secret Force of the Universe</u>, 2008

The Universal Calibration Lattice® is a system within the human energy anatomy, radiating from the very core of our being - a unique geometric and harmonic configuration of light and sound that serves as the foundation for the next level of our personal evolution. More information is available at Peggy Phoenix Dubro's website www.emfworldwide.com

Peggy also has a wonderful program for young adults called *LatticeLogic™ for Children*:

In Peggy's words, it is "a cutting-edge technology in understanding the way human beings think and function, which teaches individuals how to organize their thoughts, understandings and beliefs. This learning changes their actions and maximizes their potentials both in their personal lives and as valuable members of their communities." More information is available at her website: www.emfworldwide.com

Grotto 105:

The Institute of HeartMath at www.heartmath.org sponsors the publication of <u>The HeartMath Solution</u> by Doc Childre & Howard Martin, 1999.

Miscellaneous Out of the Box Sources:

The *Kindred Spirit* is the definitive magazine for metaphysical information. It is published in the UK and is available at www.kindredspirit.co.uk

ODE is an uplifting magazine for the Intelligent Optimist and in line with the philosophy of the Wizard's Handbook. Originating in the Netherlands, it is now available at www.odemagazine.com

And do not forget our website; it is an adventure unto itself: www.muhlatonschoolofwizardry.com

The website also links to the *Wizard's Emporium* where you can obtain interesting products as well as prints of the illustrations from the ***Wizard's Handbook***.

Be MORE Than You Can Be!

About the Author

Mario Garnet, a Rosicrucian student of Mysticism for over 45 years and a '94 graduate of Jean Houston's Mystery School is a practicing mechanical engineer and business executive. He has a B.S. in Aeronautical Engineering from Rensselaer Polytechnic Institute and an MBA from Widener University. He has had careers in government, the medical world, corporate America, and independent consulting firms, and has published several computer books.

Mario originated from Germany of Hungarian and German descent, and lived in Japan and various areas of the United States while his father completed a career in the US Army. Subsequently he has experienced many cultures outside of Europe including those of Saudi Arabia, Thailand, Egypt, Korea, Sri Lanka, Mexico, and India.

Mario lives in New Jersey with his wife Pat and stepson Steve, shares the joys of two granddaughters who live in Minnesota, and still loves to visit exotic restaurants!

Made in the USA
Lexington, KY
23 November 2016